English through the News Media

―2024 Edition―

Masami Takahashi
Noriko Itoh
Richard Powell

Asahi Press

記事提供
The New York Times
BBC News
The Asahi Shimbun
The Economist
The Japan Times
The Toronto Star
AP
Kyodo
The Guardian
AFP-JIJI

写真提供
アフロ：Redux／AFP／毎日新聞社／AP／
ロイター／MeijiShowa／MEXSPORT／
REX／Everett Collection／
新華社

地図・イラスト
ヨシオカユリ

English through the News Media —2024 Edition—
Copyright © 2024 by Asahi Press

は　し　が　き

　本書は、世界のニュースを通して Reading, Listening, Speaking, Writing のバランスのとれた学習が効果的にできるように工夫してあります。2022年12月：日本がスペインに大金星　新ページを開く；際ど過ぎる決勝ゴール判定が論争の的に、2023年1月：ナイジェリアの学校で母語使用禁止　違反者はムチ打ちの罰；AIチャットボット出現で、大学は教育方法の見直し；中南米のコカイン・カルテルと欧州、3月：イランが通貨危機に直面　その理由は？；「寿司テロ」により、回転寿司のレーンが停止；中国政府高官の多くは欧米の学校出身；カズオ・イシグロ　巨匠黒澤明監督作品をリメイク；インドネシア実習生が東日本大震災被災地の漁業を支える；AUKUSの潜水艦に関する協定は地域集団安全保障の柱；コロナウイルスの起源を巡る政治的闘い；決勝戦が日米対決となり、世界中が既に大盛り上がり；地熱発電が日本で進展しない理由；ベートーヴェンの遺髪をDNA検査　その結果は？；日本　WBC優勝に沸く；バリ島　ロシアとウクライナからの避難民受け入れ見直し；レバノンでサマータイムを巡り大混乱；スコットランドでイスラム教徒の首相誕生　英国の政治的多様性、4月：フィンランドのNATO加盟発表とロシア国境；中国を拒否し続ける台湾同盟国；大阪の「飲食店テロ」で2人逮捕；米国の驚異的な経済記録からの教訓；インドは人口で中国を追い抜く　果たして経済では？；関東大震災時の「災害映像」発見；ニュージーランド　「国王」戴冠式とマオリの人たち；アニメに救われ、イタリア人が日本で精神科医に、5月：オーストラリア　「国王」戴冠式に無関心な理由、まで世界中のニュースを満載しております。

　The New York Times, BBC News, The Asahi Shimbun, The Economist, The Japan Times, The Toronto Star, The Guardian から社会・文化・政治経済・情報・言語・教育・科学・医学・環境・娯楽・スポーツなどのあらゆる分野を網羅しましたので、身近に世界中のニュースに触れ、読み、聞き、話し、書く楽しさを育みながら、多角的にそして複眼的に英語運用力が自然に培われるように意図しています。

　24課より構成され、各課に新聞や雑誌の記事読解前にBefore you readを設けました。本文の内容が予想できる写真と、どこにあるかを示す地図と国の情報を参照しながら自由に意見交換をします。次の Words and Phrases では、記事に記載されている単語や熟語とそれに合致する英語の説明を選び、あらかじめ大事な語の理解を深めて行きます。Summaryでは記事の内容を予想しながら、5語を適当な箇所に記入して要約文を完成させます。記事読解前では難しいようであれば、読解後に活用しても良いと思います。さらに、記事に関連した裏話も載せました。記事の読解にあたり、わかり易い註釈を記事の右端に付け、理解度をチェックするための Multiple Choice, True or False, 記事に関連した語法を学ぶVocabularyと豊富に取り揃えました。Summaryと記事がそのまま音

声化されたファイルをウェブ上にあげています。多方面に渡る記事やExercisesを活用して、英字新聞に慣れ親しみ、使っていただけることを望んでいます。

　今回テキスト作成に際して、お世話になりました朝日出版社社長小川洋一郎氏、取締役部長朝日英一郎氏、編集部の新井京さんに心からお礼申し上げます。

2023年10月

高橋　優身

伊藤　典子

Richard Powell

CONTENTS

＊印の15章を *15 Selected Units of English through the News Media —2024 Edition—* として別途刊行しています。

English through the News Media -2024 Edition-

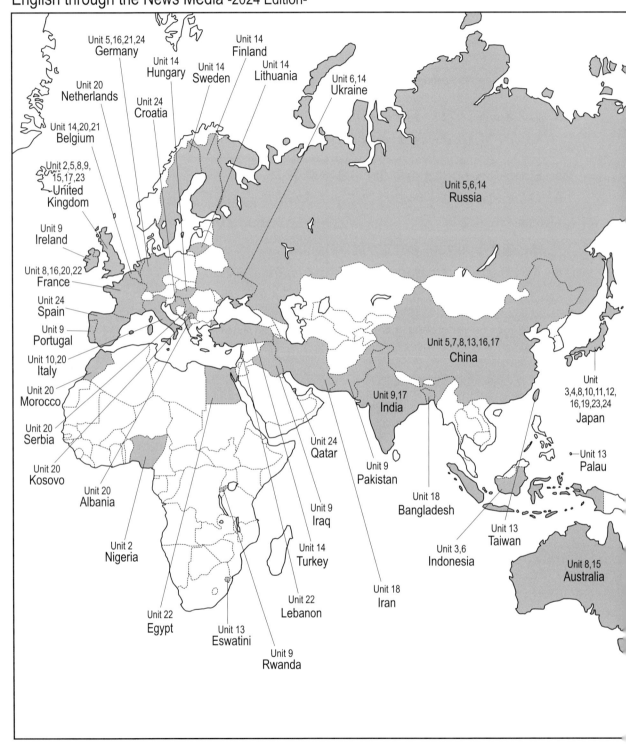

Unit 5,16,21,24 Germany

Unit 14 Finland

Unit 14 Hungary

Unit 14 Sweden

Unit 14 Lithuania

Unit 6,14 Ukraine

Unit 20 Netherlands

Unit 24 Croatia

Unit 14,20,21 Belgium

Unit 2,5,8,9, 15,17,23 United Kingdom

Unit 5,6,14 Russia

Unit 9 Ireland

Unit 8,16,20,22 France

Unit 24 Spain

Unit 9 Portugal

Unit 10,20 Italy

Unit 5,7,8,13,16,17 China

Unit 20 Morocco

Unit 20 Serbia

Unit 9,17 India

Unit 3,4,8,10,11,12, 16,19,23,24 Japan

Unit 20 Kosovo

Unit 24 Qatar

Unit 13 Palau

Unit 20 Albania

Unit 9 Pakistan

Unit 9 Iraq

Unit 18 Bangladesh

Unit 13 Taiwan

Unit 2 Nigeria

Unit 14 Turkey

Unit 3,6 Indonesia

Unit 8,15 Australia

Unit 22 Egypt

Unit 22 Lebanon

Unit 18 Iran

Unit 13 Eswatini

Unit 9 Rwanda

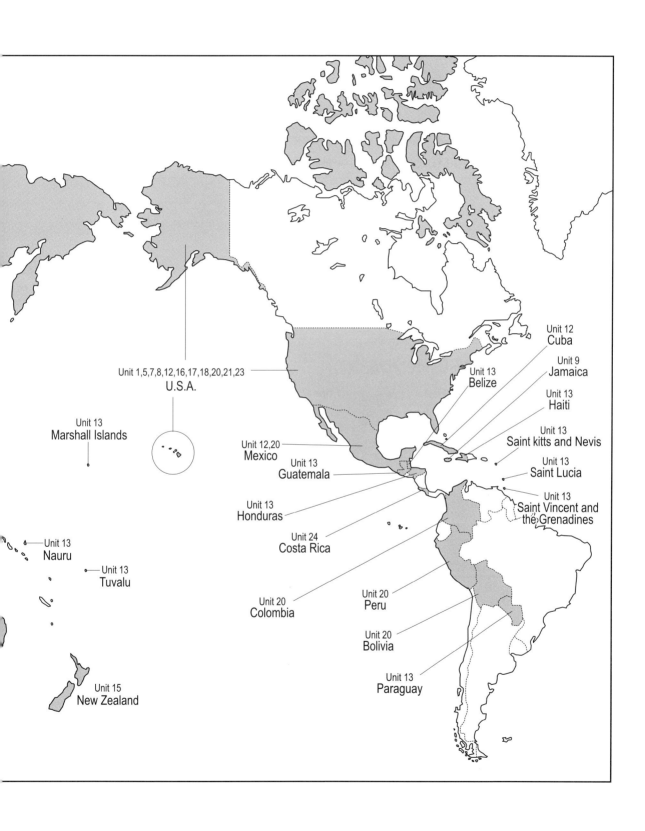

Unit 12
Cuba

Unit 9
Jamaica

Unit 13
Belize

Unit 13
Haiti

Unit 13
Saint kitts and Nevis

Unit 1,5,7,8,12,16,17,18,20,21,23
U.S.A.

Unit 13
Saint Lucia

Unit 13
Marshall Islands

Unit 13
Saint Vincent and
the Grenadines

Unit 12,20
Mexico

Unit 13
Guatemala

Unit 13
Honduras

Unit 24
Costa Rica

Unit 13
Nauru

Unit 13
Tuvalu

Unit 20
Colombia

Unit 20
Peru

Unit 20
Bolivia

Unit 13
Paraguay

Unit 15
New Zealand

音声再生アプリ「リスニング・トレーナー」を使った 音声ダウンロード

朝日出版社開発のアプリ、「リスニング・トレーナー（リストレ）」を使えば、教科書の音声を スマホ、タブレットに簡単にダウンロードできます。どうぞご活用ください。

◉ アプリ【リスニング・トレーナー】の使い方

《アプリのダウンロード》

App Store または Google Play から 「リスニング・トレーナー」のアプリ （無料）をダウンロード

App Storeは こちら▶ 　　Google Playは こちら▶

《アプリの使い方》

① アプリを開き「コンテンツを追加」をタップ
② 画面上部に【15712】を入力しDoneをタップ

音声ストリーミング配信 》》》

この教科書の音声は、 右記ウェブサイトにて 無料で配信しています。 https://text.asahipress.com/free/english/

English through the News Media

●AI チャットボット出現で、大学は教育方法の見直し

米国ゲインズビルのフロリダ大学。学生による ChatGPT 利用が急増中

写真：TODD ANDERSON ／ Redux ／アフロ

Before you read

Questions

1. What do you think the article will be about?

   この記事は何の話題についてだと思いますか？

2. What do you think about A.I. chatbots?

   AI チャットボットについてどう思いますか？

次の1～5の語句の説明として最も近いものをa～eから1つ選び、（　　）内に記入しなさい。

1. grade （　　）
2. essay （　　）
3. confess （　　）
4. overhaul （　　）
5. phase out （　　）

a. admit or acknowledge
b. redesign
c. steadily get rid of
d. written assignment
e. evaluate students' work

次の英文は記事の要約です。下の語群から最も適切な語を1つ選び、（　　）内に記入しなさい。

　While many high schools have (　　　　) A.I. tools like ChatGPT to prevent cheating, universities have been (　　　　) to do so. Instead, professors are changing their teaching (　　　　). Changes include using more in-class oral exams, group work and (　　　　) assessments. A.I. companies themselves are trying to develop technology to help teachers (　　　　) machine-generated texts.

banned　　detect　　handwritten　　methods　　reluctant

　AIチャットボットとは、データやログを基に自己学習したAIが質問に対して回答するプログラムである。Chat「おしゃべり」、Bot「ロボット」のことで、自動でチャットを行うプログラムのことである。ユーザーが自然言語で質問した内容に対して的確な返答をする。データやログが不十分な場合は、返答の精度は高くないが、データやログが蓄積されるにつれて、人間と話しているかのような自然な対話に近くなり、簡単な雑談やおしゃべりも可能になる。

　AIチャットボットは自動学習によって回答精度が次第に向上していき、より充実した回答が可能になるため、カスタマーセンターなどの問い合わせへの対応に用いられている。問い合わせ内容も複雑化していくため、AIチャットボットであれば、蓄積されたデータを基に、最適と考えられる回答を自動学習により導き出すことができ、柔軟な回答を得ることが可能である。その結果、問い合わせ対応が効率化し、待たせる時間の短縮に繋がり、さらに、回答に対する満足度も向上し、信頼性の向上も期待できる。人が対応することなく問い合わせ対応が完了し、人的コストの削減に繋がる。しかし、不適切な発言や情報が拡散する危険性もあるので、注意を払う必要がある。

Reading

1-03

Alarmed by A.I. Chatbots, Universities Start Revamping How They Teach

While grading essays for his world religions course last month, Antony Aumann, a professor of philosophy at Northern Michigan University, read what he said was easily "the best paper in the class." It explored the morality of burqa bans with
5 clean paragraphs, fitting examples and rigorous arguments.

A red flag instantly went up.

Mr. Aumann confronted his student over whether he had written the essay himself. The student confessed to using ChatGPT, a chatbot that delivers information, explains
10 concepts and generates ideas in simple sentences — and, in this case, had written the paper.

1-04

Alarmed by his discovery, Mr. Aumann decided to transform essay writing for his courses this semester. He plans to require students to write first drafts in the classroom,
15 using browsers that monitor and restrict computer activity. Mr. Aumann, who may forgo essays in subsequent semesters, also plans to weave ChatGPT into lessons by asking students to evaluate the chatbot's responses.

Across the country, university professors like Mr. Aumann,
20 department chairs and administrators are starting to overhaul classrooms in response to ChatGPT, prompting a potentially huge shift in teaching and learning. Some professors are redesigning their courses entirely, making changes that include more oral exams, group work and handwritten assessments in
25 lieu of typed ones.

1-05

The moves are part of a real-time grappling with a new technological wave known as generative artificial intelligence. ChatGPT, which was released in November by the artificial intelligence lab OpenAI, is at the forefront of the shift.
30 The chatbot generates eerily articulate and nuanced text in response to short prompts, with people using it to write love letters, poetry, fan fiction — and their schoolwork.

That has upended some middle and high schools, with

A.I. : 生成 AI（人工知能）
Chatbots : 対話型 AI（種類名）
essays : レポート
course : 講義科目
easily : 問題なく
burqa : ブルカ《イスラム教徒の女性が外出時に着用する全身を覆うベール》
arguments : 論拠
ChatGPT : チャット GPT《アプリ名》
generates 〜 : 〜を生成する
forgo 〜 : 〜を控える、断念する
weave 〜 into … : 〜を…に織り込む
department chairs : 学科長
shift : 変化
assessments : 評価
in lieu of 〜 : 〜の代わりに
grappling with 〜 : 〜に取り組む
OpenAI :《企業名》
fan fiction : 二次創作物語、サイドストーリー
upended 〜 : 〜に強烈な影響を与えた

teachers and administrators trying to discern whether students
35 are using the chatbot to do their schoolwork. Some public
school systems, including in New York City and Seattle,
have since banned the tool on school Wi-Fi networks and
devices to prevent cheating, though students can easily find
workarounds to access ChatGPT.

cheating：不正行為

workarounds：回避策

1-06

40   In higher education, colleges and universities have been
reluctant to ban the A.I. tool because administrators doubt
the move would be effective and they don't want to infringe
on academic freedom. That means the way people teach is
changing instead.

infringe on ～：～を侵害する

45   OpenAI is expected to soon release another tool, GPT-
4, which is better at generating text than previous versions.
Google has built LaMDA, a rival chatbot, and Microsoft is
discussing a $10 billion investment in OpenAI. Silicon Valley
start-ups, including StabilityAI and Character AI, are also
50 working on generative A.I. tools.

LaMDA：《アプリ名》

Silicon Valley：シリコンバレー《IT企業の集積地》

start-ups：新興企業

StabilityAI：《企業名》

Character AI：《企業名》

1-07   An OpenAI spokeswoman said the lab recognized its
programs could be used to mislead people and was developing
technology to help people identify text generated by ChatGPT.

At schools including George Washington University in
55 Washington, D.C., Rutgers University in New Brunswick, N.J.,
and Appalachian State University in Boone, N.C., professors
are phasing out take-home, open-book assignments — which
became a dominant method of assessment in the pandemic
but now seem vulnerable to chatbots. They are instead opting
60 for in-class assignments, handwritten papers, group work and
oral exams.

N.J.：ニュージャージー州

Appalachian State University：州立アパラチア大学

N.C.：ノースカロライナ州

phasing out ～：～を段階的に廃止する

assignments：課題

vulnerable to ～：～に対して脆弱な

Kalley Huang
The New York Times, January 16, 2023

Exercises

Multiple Choice

次の 1 ～ 5 の英文の質問に答えるために、 a ～ d の中から最も適切なものを 1 つ選びなさい。

1. What prompted Professor Aumann to revamp his essay writing course?

    a. He was looking for a more efficient way to grade papers.

    b. He wanted students to make more use of chatbots.

    c. He had been planning to overhaul his classroom for some time.

    d. He discovered a student used A.I. to write an essay.

2. What is ChatGPT?

    a. A chatbot that monitors student computer activity.

    b. An A.I. tool that generates text.

    c. A program that detects if a text was written by A.I..

    d. A chatbot built by Google.

3. Why are some public schools banning ChatGPT?

    a. To prevent cheating.

    b. To discourage students from wasting money.

    c. To encourage group work.

    d. To phase out take-home assignments.

4. Why are many colleges and universities reluctant to ban A.I.?

    a. They have invested heavily in A.I. technology.

    b. They want to protect academic freedom.

    c. They believe it writes better essays than students do.

    d. They do not care if students cheat.

5. What is OpenAI doing to address concerns about ChatGPT?

    a. Banning it from schools and universities.

    b. Developing technology to help people identify A.I.-generated texts.

    c. Ignoring the criticism made by teachers.

    d. Collaborating with Microsoft and Google.

本文の内容に合致するものに T（True）、合致しないものに F（False）をつけなさい。

(   ) **1.** ChatGPT creates new concepts and complex ideas.

(   ) **2.** Students can use a chatbot to do their homework.

(   ) **3.** Colleges and universities seem likely to ban the A.I. tool.

(   ) **4.** OpenAI and Google have just built LaMDA.

(   ) **5.** Administrators who work at universities want to reduce academic freedom.

Vocabulary

次の 1 ～ 7 は、A.I.（artificial intelligence）に関する語句です。下の a ～ g の説明文の中から最も適切なものを 1 つ選び、（　）内に記入しなさい。

1. app   (   )
2. ChatGPT   (   )
3. A.I.   (   )
4. smartphone   (   )
5. tablet   (   )
6. drone   (   )
7. chatbot   (   )

a. a mobile phone that can be used as a small computer and that connects to the internet

b. a shortening of the term "application software"

c. personal computer used by tapping with a finger on a touch screen

d. an application that interacts in a conversational way and generates text

e. the ability of a computer program to think and learn, and also a field of study which tries to make computers smart

f. an aircraft without a pilot that is controlled by someone on the ground

g. a robot that can respond to spoken or written questions from people

●ナイジェリアの学校で母語使用禁止

違反者はムチ打ちの罰

ナイジェリア南西部オグン州イバフォにある私立学校での授業指導の様子。公立学校より良質の私立学校に子供を通わせる親が増えている。　　写真：AFP／アフロ

Before you read

Federal Republic of Nigeria
ナイジェリア連邦共和国

面積　923,773km²（日本の約2.5倍）（世界31位）
人口　206,140,000人（世界7位）
公用語　英語、ハウサ語、ヨルバ語、イボ語など
首都　アブジャ
最大都市　ラゴス
民族　ハウサ、ヨルバ、イボなど500以上の民族・部族
宗教　イスラム教・シーア派　50%（北部）、
　　　キリスト教　40%（南部）、伝統宗教（全域）
GDP　4,323億ドル
　　　1人当たり GNI　2,000ドル
通貨　ナイラ
政体　連邦共和制（大統領制）
識字率　68%

Words and Phrases

次の1～5の語の説明として最も近いものをa～eから1つ選び、（　）内に記入しなさい。

1. stumped （　）
2. reprimand （　）
3. tide （　）
4. comprehension （　）
5. decipher （　）

a. understanding
b. criticism, scolding
c. decode, interpret
d. trend
e. unable to answer

Summary

次の英文は記事の要約です。下の語群から最も適切な語を1つ選び、（　）内に記入しなさい。

1-08

60 years after independence, English remains Nigeria's (　　　) language. A new language policy will require (　　　) instruction for the first six years of school. But implementing this will be (　　　) in a country of over 625 languages. (　　　) a teacher once beaten for using his mother tongue thinks schools have no (　　　) but to teach mainly in English.

challenging   choice   even   mother-tongue   official

　　ナイジェリア連邦共和国は、アフリカ大陸西南部に位置する連邦制和国で、人口は2億1,140万人。イギリス連邦加盟国の1国でもある。ナイジェリアの地には過去数千年間に多数の王国や部族国家が存在してきたが、現在のナイジェリア連邦共和国の源流は、19世紀以来の英国による植民地支配と、1914年の南北部ナイジェリア保護領の合併にもとめられる。1960年に正式に独立し、1967年から1970年にかけて内戦に陥った。
　　若年人口は世界でも非常に多く、多民族国家とみなされており、500を超えるエスニック・グループを擁する。北部のハウサ人およびフラニ人が全人口の29%、南西部のヨルバ人が21%、南東部のイボ人が18%。彼らの言語も500を超え、文化の違いも多岐にわたっている。方言を含め521の言語が確認されているが、政府は625もあるのではないかと推測している。議会や官庁でおもに使用される事実上の公用語は英語であるが、議会ではハウサ語、ヨルバ語、イボ語の使用が認められている。初等教育では母語によって授業が行われるが、高等教育においては英語のみを使用している。宗教はおおまかに南部のキリスト教と北部のイスラム教に二分される。ナイジェリアは人口と経済規模から「アフリカの巨人」と称されている。

Reading

1-09

Nigerian schools: Flogged for speaking my mother tongue

Kareem*, whose mother tongue is Yoruba, was just a secondary school student when he was whipped in class for not speaking in English.

"When I was growing up, I was struggling to speak
5 English," he tells the BBC. "There was a particular class," he says, recalling the incident in 2010. The teacher called him up to answer a question, and he was stumped.

"I know the answer but I can only respond with my mother language," he remembers saying.

10 His was not an isolated incident he says, and other students at his school received harsh reprimands for daring to speak in Yoruba instead of English.

1-10

More than 60 years after independence from Britain, English remains Nigeria's official language, and is used in
15 public settings such as schools, universities, government and many work places.

But the political tide appears to be turning. In November, Education Minister Adamu Adamu announced the National Language Policy which stipulates that the first six years of
20 primary education should be taught in the children's mother tongue.

He said the changes were necessary because pupils learn better when they are taught in "their own mother tongue."

Currently, primary school children are taught in English,
25 with teachers in certain communities mixing local languages with English for ease of comprehension.

However, it is unclear how the new policy will be rolled out because — in a country where government estimates say 625 different languages are spoken, and with people moving
30 around the country — many Nigerian children live in areas where their mother tongue is not the dominant local language.

Flogged for 〜：〜してムチで打たれる
mother tongue：母語

＊BBC News の指示に従い、名前を省略
Yoruba：ヨルバ語《西アフリカのニジェール・主流語族に属する言語》
whipped for 〜：〜してムチで打たれる
BBC：英国放送協会
particular：（ナイジェリア）特有の
recalling 〜：〜を思い出す
incident：出来事
stumped：困惑した
reprimands：叱責
daring to 〜：敢えて〜する

public settings：公共の場

stipulates 〜：〜を規定する

comprehension：理解
rolled out：展開される
estimates：推計

dominant：支配的な

Teaching in the mother tongue was in fact first put forward as a national policy in the 1970s, but because of difficulties rolling it out in such a linguistically diverse country, it was
35 never put into effect, as the government wishes to do now.

1-12

The policy is already facing stiff opposition. Despite his own experience, Kareem, who is now a school teacher, does not think teaching in local languages is a good idea.

"If you were to take a look at Nigeria as a country, we have
40 more than 500 languages, which will make it very hard" to implement.

He questions how classes could be taught properly in a local language when it may contain students who speak different tongues at home. In his own class in Sabongidda-
45 Ora, in the southern Edo State, five different languages are spoken, he says - Igbo, Yoruba, Hausa, Ora and Esan.

1-13

Although he is supposed to teach in English, there are times when he has to explain things in Pidgeon English, so all the pupils can understand.

50 "There's no point in teaching them something they cannot decipher, it would be very wrong."

However, "I can't be teaching students in their local language" he insists, because he simply does not know how to speak all the various tongues spoken by his students.

55 Furthermore, if they don't speak English in primary school, they will find it difficult later on, he adds.

Cecilia Macaulay
BBC News, January 7, 2023

put forward：提唱される

put into effect：実施される

stiff opposition：強い反対

implement：実施する

is supposed to ～：～する
ことになっている

Pidgeon English：ピジョン
英語《東南アジアや南西
太平洋諸国で用いられる、
英語と現地語との混成語》

no point in ～：～しても意
味が無い

decipher：解読する

Exercises

Multiple Choice

次の１の英文を完成させ、２〜５の英文の質問に答えるために、ａ〜ｄの中から最も適切なものを１つ選びなさい。

1. The new National Language Policy announced by Adamu Adamu is to
   a. replace English with Yoruba as Nigeria's official language.
   b. instruct children in English from an early age.
   c. teach children in their mother tongue for the first six years of primary education.
   d. educate children in a mix of English and their mother tongue.

2. Why does Kareem disagree with the policy?
   a. He wants more children to learn his mother tongue.
   b. Most children really want to study English.
   c. It is not practical in such a linguistically diverse country.
   d. He fears that children would get beaten for speaking English.

3. What is Kareem's occupation?
   a. Minister of Education.
   b. School teacher.
   c. University professor of Yoruba.
   d. Education officer in southern Edo State.

4. According to the article, what problem might result from teaching in a local language?
   a. Children coming from another area might not understand it.
   b. There could be a shortage of books in that language.
   c. Igbo-speaking pupils might argue with Yoruba-speaking pupils.
   d. Nigeria could lose its status as a former British colony.

5. How many languages are spoken in Sabongidda-Ora?
   a. At least 5.
   b. More than 50.
   c. Around 500.
   d. About 625.

本文の内容に合致するものにＴ（True）、合致しないものにＦ（False）をつけなさい。

(   ) **1.** Kareem teaches in the eastern Edo State.

(   ) **2.** More than 621 languages are spoken in Nigeria.

(   ) **3.** The Nigerian Language Policy states that primary schools should teach children in their mother tongues.

(   ) **4.** Adamu Adamu said he had a hard time speaking English at school.

(   ) **5.** Igbo is one of five different languages spoken in Sabongidda-Ora.

Vocabulary

次の１〜10 は、「話す」に関する英文です。日本文に合うように、say, speak, talk, tell から最も適切な語を１つ選び、必要なときは形を変えて、（   ）内に記入しなさい。

1. 同僚の間で評判が良くない。
You are not well (   ) of by your colleagues.

2. 明後日までにこの本を読むように言われた。
I was (   ) to finish reading this book by the day after tomorrow.

3. 世間はうるさいものだ。
People will (   ).

4. 彼女は世界一の歌手だと言っても過言ではない。
It is not too much to (   ) that she is the greatest singer in the world.

5. あなたが述べたことは、誠実さを示している。
What you said (   ) for your sincerity.

6. 彼女がパーティに来るのはもちろんだ。
It goes without (   ) that she is coming to the party.

7. あの少年グループが次に何をしでかすか分かったものではない。
There is no (   ) what that group of boys will do next.

8. 厳密に言うと、私は女優に向いていない。
Strictly (   ), I am not cut out to be an actress.

9. 彼は信頼できる男だと言える。
It can be (   ) that he is a reliable man.

10. 訳の分からないことを言わないで。
Don't (   ) nonsense.

●インドネシア実習生が東日本大震災被災地の漁業を
支える

宮城県沖の底引き網漁船で、日本人の同僚と魚の選別をするインドネシアの技能実習生

写真：毎日新聞社／アフロ

Before you read

Republic of Indonesia
インドネシア共和国

面積	1,920,000km²（日本の約5倍）（世界15位）
人口	270,000,000人（世界4位）
首都	ジャカルタ
公用語	インドネシア語
識字率	88.5%
民族	ジャワ人　45%／スンダ人　14%／マドゥラ人　7.5%
	沿岸マレー人　7.5%／中国系　5%／その他　21%
宗教	イスラム教　86.7%、キリスト教　10.72%
	ヒンズー教　1.74%、仏教　0.77%
GDP	1兆596億3,800万ドル（世界15位）
	1人当たりGDP　3,922ドル
通貨	ルピア
政体	大統領制・共和制

Words and Phrases

次の1～5の語句の説明として最も近いものをa～eから1つ選び、（　）内に記入しなさい。

1. unaccustomed　（　　）
2. crewmate　（　　）
3. dependent　（　　）
4. alleviating　（　　）
5. prop up　（　　）

a. unfamiliar
b. team member
c. support
d. relying
e. easing

Summary

次の英文は記事の要約です。下の語群から最も適切な語を1つ選び、（　）内に記入しなさい。

1-14

　　Indonesians are helping keep Tohoku's (　　　　　　) industry alive. The 2011 tsunami worsened a growing (　　　　　　) shortage. So in 2013 a program was (　　　　　　) to train foreign fishermen. To improve (　　　　　), boat owners visit the parents of Indonesian interns. Moreover, interns take part in local cultural activities that could (　　　　　) not continue because of lack of manpower.

fishing　　implemented　　integration　　labor　　otherwise

　　「開発途上国の人材育成を通した国際貢献」を目的に、1993年に技能実習が制度化された。しかし、実際はその目的とはかけ離れ、過重労働や違法な労働条件、賃金未払い、職場での暴力やいじめなど多くの問題が発生している。原則的に職場を変更できないため、過酷な状況に耐えきれず多くの技能実習生が失踪し、2021年で約7000人以上にもなる。
　　外国人労働者、特に東南アジアの人々に対する偏見や間違った認識によって、技能実習生を「安く雇える労働者」と見なしている。国際貢献という名のもと、低コストで外国人労働者を確保しようとする経済界の体質も大きな問題だ。技能実習生＝安い労働者という価値観を持ったまま、受け入れ企業に仲介している。そのため、受け入れ企業は理解不足と、「安い労働者」という認識で技能実習生を扱い、違法労働や人権侵害の問題が発生しやすい状況になっている。受け入れ側と技能実習生の相互の信頼と理解は重要だ。就労前にきちんと技能実習制度の内容や労働条件などについて話し合い、単なる労働者ではなく、働く仲間として受け入れ、相互理解できるように時間をかけるべきだ。

Reading

1-15

Indonesian interns keep fisheries afloat in city hit by 3/11

ISHINOMAKI, Miyagi Prefecture — Early on a chilly mid-February morning, high waves rocked a fishing boat so fiercely that anyone unaccustomed to the erratic motions would have immediately gotten seasick.

5　　Prana Firnagis, 25, who came to Japan about four years ago from his native Indonesia to work as one of the 16 technical interns at the Yamane Gyogyobu fisheries company, checked to make sure the sudden shock was not too much for his crewmates to handle.

10　　Young trainees then leaned out of the vessel to collect cod and Japanese sea bass with hooks, haul them onto the deck and put ice on them.

　　Communities along the Sanriku coast, including this one, became increasingly dependent on foreign workers like this ship's crew in rebuilding the fisheries and seafood processing industries after the 2011 Great East Japan Earthquake and tsunami.

　　The rural Oshika district here, for example, saw its population plummet to 2,000 from 4,500 after it was razed by the earthquake and tsunami 12 years ago, with elderly citizens making up more than 50 percent of those who remained.

　　Ishinomaki city had signed an agreement with the West Java provincial government in Indonesia way back in 2007 to accept technical interns in the hopes of alleviating the labor shortage and the aging workforce.

　　Residents of Ishinomaki initially found it difficult to get along with newcomers.

　　But as depopulated communities along the Oshika Peninsula like this one become increasingly difficult to maintain, the young laborers brought in from outside Japan are finding ways to fit in with the locals. And some of the efforts by area residents may

1-16

1-17

interns：実習生

keep ～ afloat：～を支える

3/11：東日本大震災

ISHINOMAKI：石巻市《本社以外の地から送られた記事の配信地名》

unaccustomed to ～：～に慣れていない

erratic：不規則な

Yamane Gyogyobu：山根漁業部《株式会社名》

leaned out of ～：～から身を乗り出した

cod：タラ

Japanese sea bass：スズキ

dependent on ～：～に頼る

seafood processing industries：水産加工業

Oshika district：牡鹿地区

plummet to ～：～に激減する

signed an agreement with ～：～と協定を結んだ

way back：ずっと昔の

alleviating ～：～を緩和させる

get along with ～：～と仲良くする

fit in with ～：～と溶け込む

16 Unit 3

offer other cities lessons learned for how to prop up Japan's aging society and shrinking workforce.

Local fishing boat owners began to visit the parents of Indonesian interns every year to help them feel at ease even after their children leave their family homes for Japan.

A "scholarship" program was put in place in 2013 for training fishermen. Ship owners provide funds for youth in Indonesia to take Japanese language classes and obtain qualifications needed for working in the fisheries industry.

Last summer, a mosque was completed at the base of the peninsula.

On the very edge of the Oshika Peninsula projecting out to the Pacific, the Ayukawahama district with its population of about 660 hosts some 40 Indonesians who came here to work in one of the world's most fertile fishing grounds.

But the interns' lives here extend into other key community activities far beyond work.

Hidenori Ando, 72, the shrine's chief priest, said he started asking local fisheries to send him non-Japanese carriers of a "mikoshi" portable shrine seven years ago, when the festival finally resumed after pausing in the wake of the disaster.

"It is no longer possible for Japanese people alone to carry the portable shrine," Ando said.

Now, a photo of Aldi Wandiri, 23, and other young people from Indonesia carrying a portable shrine is printed on a leaflet promoting the local festival.

Ryuichiro Fukuoka
The Asahi Shimbun Asia & Japan Watch, March 13, 2023

prop up 〜：〜を支える

feel at ease：安心する

put in place：導入される

qualifications：資格

mosque：モスク《イスラム教礼拝所》

at the base of 〜：〜の付け根に

projecting out to 〜：〜に突き出た

Ayukawahama：鮎川浜地区

hosts 〜：〜が住んでいる

extend into 〜：〜まで及ぶ

chief priest：宮司

in the wake of 〜：〜の結果

leaflet：パンフレット

Exercises

Multiple Choice

次の１～２の英文を完成させ、３～５の英文の質問に答えるために、ａ～ｄの中から最も適切なものを１つ選びなさい。

1. To help reassure the families of the young interns, some Japanese locals

    a. provided them with funds for language classes.

    b. constructed a mosque at the Yamane Gyogyobu company.

    c. went all the way to Indonesia to visit them.

    d. sent them to work in the fisheries industry.

2. A local Shinto priest asked for help from local fisheries because he

    a. found that Japanese people had lost interest in local customs.

    b. needed Indonesian interns to help support a local festival.

    c. wanted to improve relations between the Shinto and Muslim religions.

    d. needed to repair the portable shrine after the tsunami.

3. What is the main reason for the influx of foreign workers to Sanriku?

    a. Rapid depopulation in the area.

    b. A local desire to help young people in poorer countries.

    c. The high cost of labor after the 2011 tsunami.

    d. The high cost of rebuilding infrastructure damaged by the tsunami.

4. What is the main purpose of the scholarship program?

    a. To provide technical training for young Japanese fishermen.

    b. To offer lessons on how to manage Japan's aging society.

    c. To teach about Japanese culture so that interns can integrate better.

    d. To help Indonesians learn Japanese and gain fishing qualifications.

5. Why did Ishinomaki sign an agreement with an Indonesian province?

    a. To help rebuild areas damaged by the 2011 disaster.

    b. To bring in more workers to support the local economy.

    c. To boost the export of seafood and other local products.

    d. To acquire knowledge of Indonesian fishing technology.

本文の内容に合致するものにＴ（True）、合致しないものにＦ（False）をつけなさい。

(   ) **1.** Indonesian interns came to Japan in order to help the Sanriku fisheries industry.

(   ) **2.** Indonesian interns are encouraged to learn about both the Japanese language and also fisheries.

(   ) **3.** Mosques have been built for Indonesian trainees at the base of the peninsula.

(   ) **4.** Young people make up of more than 50% of residents in rural Oshika.

(   ) **5.** Hidenori Ando is researching connections between Japanese culture and Indonesian culture.

Vocabulary

次の１〜７は、「fish 魚」に関することわざです。下の語群の中から最も適切な語を１つ選び、（   ）内に、また下の最も適切なａ〜ｇの和文の中から１つ選び、[   ]内に記入しなさい。

1. All is fish that comes to the (   ). [   ]

2. We have other fish to (   ). [   ]

3. I felt like a fish out of (   ). [   ]

4. There are (   ) more fish in the sea. [   ]

5. He is a (   ) fish in a small pond. [   ]

6. The best fish (   ) when they are three days old. [   ]

7. (   ) fish are big. [   ]

| big | fry | missed | net | plenty | smell | water |

a. まるで陸に上がったカッパのようだ。
b. 井の中の蛙だ。
c. 客も３日もいれば鼻につく。
d. 利用できるものは何でも利用する。
e. 逃げた魚は大きい。
f. チャンスはいくらもある。
g. 他に大事な仕事がある。

●地熱発電が日本で進展しない理由

熊本県小国町の「わいたグリーンエナジー地熱発電所」全景。脱化石燃料
の流れで注目されるが、温泉旅館経営者の反対により、建設が進まない。
なぜ？

写真：Redux／アフロ

Before you read

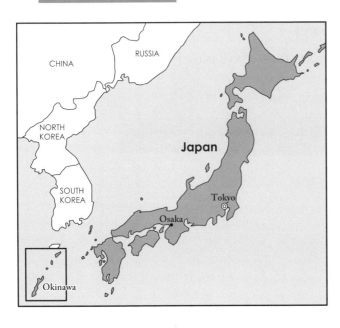

Japan
日本国

面積　377,961.73km²（世界61位）
人口　126,860,000人（世界11位）
　　　日本民族　98.5%
　　　朝鮮人　0.5%
　　　中国人　0.4%
首都　東京都
最大都市　大阪市（昼間人口）
　　　　　横浜市（夜間人口）
　　　　　東京都23区部
GDP　4兆9,718億ドル（世界3位）
　　　1人当たりのGDP　39,304ドル（世界26位）
通貨　円
公用語　なし、事実上日本語
宗教　無宗教信者　52%
　　　仏教　35%／神道　4%
　　　キリスト教　2.3%
政体　立憲君主制
識字率　99.8%

次の１～５の語の説明として最も近いものをa～eから１つ選び、（　）内に記入しなさい。

1. getaway　　　　（　）　　　　**a.** goal
2. harness　　　　（　）　　　　**b.** origin
3. abundant　　　 （　）　　　　**c.** calm, relaxing place
4. ambition　　　 （　）　　　　**d.** capture and use
5. source　　　　 （　）　　　　**e.** plenty

Summary

次の英文は記事の要約です。下の語群から最も適切な語を１つ選び、（　）内に記入しなさい。

1-20

Japan could provide 10% of its electricity from its (　　　　) geothermal resources. But it currently (　　　　) only 0.3% from them. Hot spring owners oppose new (　　　　) plants, fearing damage to their businesses and to the country's cultural (　　　　). Energy developers say there is little (　　　　) of plants affecting hot springs, but the interconnection between the two is not fully understood.

generates　　geothermal　　heritage　　risk　　vast

　　日本は、風力、太陽光、地熱のような再生可能エネルギー資源に恵まれた国だ。気候変動対策、さらにロシアのウクライナ侵攻で、エネルギー安全保障の議論が高まっている。また脱炭素へと進んでいるなか、太陽光や風力そして原発活用への議論も盛んになってきた。しかし、「地熱エネルギー資源」活用は、あまり取り上げられていない。地熱は、地中の熱を利用する再生可能エネルギーで、太陽光や風力よりも変動性が少なく、１年を通じて安定に発電できると言われている。
　　火山国である日本では、全体の地熱資源量は世界有数だと言われているが、規制やコスト、地質などさまざまな理由を前に拒まれてきた。しかし、地熱資源が復活している。アメリカの地熱資源量は3000万KW、インドネシア2779万KW、日本が2347万KWである。日本では、地熱発電の割合は１％以下で、この20年で３割減退したと言われている。2050年のカーボンニュートラルの目標を前に、政府は2030年までに、地熱発電量を４倍に引き上げる計画を掲げている。

Reading

1-21

Geothermal Power, Cheap and Clean, Could Help Run Japan. So Why Doesn't It?

A treasured getaway for travelers in Japan is a retreat to one of thousands of hot spring resorts nestled in the mountains or perched on scenic coasts, some of which have been frequented for centuries.

5　All are powered by Japan's abundant geothermal energy. In fact, Japan sits on so much geothermal energy potential, if harnessed to generate electricity, it could play a major role in replacing the nation's coal, gas or nuclear plants.

For decades, however, Japan's geothermal energy
10　ambitions have been blocked by its surprisingly powerful hot spring owners.

1-22

"Rampant geothermal development is a threat to our culture," said Yoshiyasu Sato, proprietor of Daimaru Asunaroso, a secluded inn set next to a hot spring in the
15　mountains of Fukushima Prefecture that is said to date back some 1,300 years. "If something were to happen to our onsens," he said, using the Japanese word for hot springs, "who will pay?"

Japan, an archipelago thought to sit atop the third-largest
20　geothermal resources of any country on earth, harnesses puzzlingly little of its geothermal wealth. It generates about 0.3 percent of its electricity from geothermal energy, a squandered opportunity, analysts say, for a resource-poor country that is in desperate need of new and cleaner ways of
25　generating power.

1-23

In a pre-emptive move, Mr. Sato has fit Asunaroso with monitoring equipment that tracks water flows and temperatures in real time, and is pushing for onsens across the country to do the same. He has led the opposition to geothermal development
30　as the chairman of an organization that translates loosely as the Society to Protect Japan's Secluded Hot Springs.

Geothermal Power：地熱発電
Run 〜：〜を元気にする
treasured getaway：大切ないこいの場
retreat to 〜：〜へ避難する
nestled in 〜：〜に囲まれた
perched on 〜：〜に位置する
harnessed：利用される
generate electricity：発電する
replacing 〜：〜に取って代わる
nuclear plants：原子力発電所
ambitions：野心
Daimaru Asunaroso：大丸あすなろ荘
secluded：人里離れた
set next to 〜：〜に隣接した
archipelago：群島
wealth：資産
in desperate need of 〜：〜を心底必要としている
pre-emptive move：先制措置
monitoring equipment：監視装置
Society to Protect Japan's Secluded Hot Springs：日本秘湯を守る会

Bureaucrats in Tokyo, Japan's giant electrical utilities and even the nation's manufacturing giants have been no match. "We can't forcibly push a project forward without the proper
35 understanding," said Shuji Ajima of the Tokyo-based Electric Power Development Company, also called J-Power, which operates just one geothermal plant in Japan, accounting for 0.1 percent of its power generation. The utility has been forced to give up on a number of geothermal projects in past decades.

40 "Geothermal plants are never going to be game-changers, but I believe they can still play a role in carbon-free energy," he said.

1-24

Developers say that because plants draw from sources deep beneath onsen springs, there is little possibility one will
45 affect the other.

Still, the interconnection between hot springs and deeper geothermal heat remains something of a mystery. When hot spring flows change, it's often difficult to pin down a cause.

"We don't yet fully understand the full consequences of
50 geothermal development," said Yuki Yusa, a professor emeritus and expert in geothermal sciences at Kyoto University.

1-25

Japan, the world's fifth-largest emitter of planet-warming gases, needs more clean energy to meet its climate goals and to rein in its dependence on fossil fuel imports. Much of
55 its nuclear power program remains shuttered after the 2011 Fukushima nuclear disaster.

If Japan were to develop all of its conventional geothermal resources for electricity production, it could provide about 10 percent of Japan's electricity, according to the Institute for
60 Sustainable Energy Policies in Tokyo.

Hiroko Tabuchi
The New York Times, March 22, 2023

Bureaucrats：官僚

electrical utilities：電力会社

no match：（彼には）太刀打ちできない

Electric Power Development Company：電源開発会社

accounting for ～：～を占める

draw from ～：～を利用する

interconnection：相互関係

pin down ～：～を特定する

consequences：結果

professor emeritus：名誉教授

emitter：排出国

meet ～：～を達成する

rein in ～：～を抑える

fossil fuel：化石燃料

shuttered：（業務が）終了した

nuclear disaster：原発事故

Institute for Sustainable Energy Policies：環境エネルギー政策研究所

Exercises

Multiple Choice

次の1〜4の英文の質問に答え、5の英文を完成させるために、a〜dの中から最も適切なものを1つ選びなさい。

1. How much of Japan's electricity is generated from geothermal energy?

    a. Less than half a percent.

    b. About one percent.

    c. About ten percent.

    d. More than 15 percent.

2. What does Ajima say about his company's geothermal plant?

    a. It is the first of many similar ones about to be opened by J-Power.

    b. It will become profitable as soon as it is allowed to operate.

    c. It could play a part in reducing carbon emissions.

    d. It supplies 0.1% of Tokyo's electricity.

3. How might investing in geothermal power help Japan?

    a. It could supply a third of the country's energy needs.

    b. It could help the nation meet its climate goals.

    c. It could reduce the money Japanese squander at hot spring resorts.

    d. It could speed up the reopening of all the nuclear power plants there.

4. How does Professor Yusa's view of geothermal power differ from that of its developers?

    a. He believes onsen owners will benefit from it.

    b. He would like to see more plants built.

    c. He is uncertain whether its development will affect hot springs.

    d. He argues that the water it exploits is different from hot spring water.

5. Geothermal power has been slow to expand in Japan because

    a. most bureaucrats and electrical utilities oppose it.

    b. many hot spring owners are worried about its effects.

    c. no one is interested in investing in the necessary technology.

    d. the country's dependence on fossil fuels has been reined in sufficiently.

本文の内容に合致するものにT（True）、合致しないものにF（False）をつけなさい。

(　) **1.** Japan has run out of geothermal power.

(　) **2.** Geothermal development has been blocked by the Japanese government.

(　) **3.** Geothermal energy could help take the place of the nation's nuclear plants.

(　) **4.** J-Power's geothermal plant accounts for 25% of electric-generating capacity in Japan.

(　) **5.** Geothermal plants will revolutionize Japan's energy in the near future.

Vocabulary

　次の１〜７は、「climate change 気候変動」に関する英文です。日本文に合わせて（　）内に最も適切な語を下の語群から１つ選び、記入しなさい。

1. 気候変動問題は、緊急の注意を向ける必要がある。
The (　　　　　　　　) issue requires urgent attention.

2. 地球温暖化は、人類の脅威である。
(　　　　　　　　) is a threat to mankind.

3. 水力発電は、温室効果ガスの排出量が極めて小さい。
Hydropower emits almost no (　　　　　　　　) gases.

4. 天然ガスは、化石燃料だ。
Natural gas is a (　　　　　　).

5. 我々は、二酸化炭素を削減する必要がある。
We need to reduce (　　　　　　).

6. 地熱発電は、クリーンなエネルギーとして活用が期待される。
(　　　　　　　) generation is a promising form of clean energy.

7. 50万人以上の子供たちが、いまだに栄養失調に苦しんでいる。
More than half a million children still suffer from (　　　　　　　　).

carbon dioxide	climate change	fossil fuel	geothermal power
global warming	greenhouse	malnutrition	

5

●中国政府高官の多くは欧米の学校出身

北京での国際教育博覧会。外国留学の目的は各自異なるので、留学生全員が留学先の国が好きになるとの考えは余りにも短絡的すぎないか。米国の大学が経営のために留学生を呼び込もうとしているのが現状では　写真：Mark Leong／Redux／アフロ

Before you read

People's Republic of China
中華人民共和国

面積　9,634,057km²（日本の約25倍）（世界４位）
人口　1,433,784,000人（世界１位）
首都　北京／最大都市　上海
公用語　中国語
識字率　95.9%
民族　漢族　11億7,000万〜12億人（90%〜92%）
　　　55の少数民族　8%
　　　チワン族（1,600万人）満族（1,000万人）
　　　回族（900万人）ミャオ族（800万人）
　　　ウイグル族・イ族（各700万人）ブイ族（300万人）
宗教　宗教信者　1億人　0.08%／仏教　6.2%
　　　キリスト教　2.3%／道教・無宗教　87.4%
　　　イスラム教　1.7%
GDP　13兆3,680億ドル（世界２位）
　　　1人当たりのGDP　9,580ドル（世界72位）
通貨　元
政体　一党独裁制の社会主義共和国

次の１〜５の語句の説明として最も近いものを a〜e から１つ選び、（　）内に記入しなさい。

1. squabble　　　（　　）　　　a. persuade someone to like
2. denounce　　　（　　）　　　b. increase
3. endear to　　　（　　）　　　c. condemn
4. swell　　　　　（　　）　　　d. argue
5. permeate　　　（　　）　　　e. spread through

Summary

次の英文は記事の要約です。下の語群から最も適切な語を１つ選び、（　）内に記入しなさい。

1-26

Western countries have (　　　　　) millions of Chinese students, hoping to (　　　　) future leaders to liberal values. Over 20% of Central Committee members and eight of the 24 Politburo (　　　　) studied in the West. Although China's government used to be (　　　　) of returnees, the experience does not seem to have made them pro-Western. Indeed an anti-Western spirit (　　　　) the leadership.

endear　　hosted　　members　　permeates　　suspicious

　　中国政府高官の多くは欧米諸国で教育を受けた。過去40年間に何百万人もの中国人学生が西側諸国で学んだ。西側の指導者たちは、中国の若者たちの経験が将来の中国の指導者たちに自由な価値観を惹きつけることを望んでいた。しかし、今日中国共産党は、反西洋的であり、2023年３月の全国人民代表大会での習近平主席と秦剛外相の言葉に反映されている。外国での教育を受けて中国に帰国する学生を「海外から帰国する」と言う。ところが「海外から帰国する」と「海亀」と同音異義語のため、長い間、中国の官僚機構に入った人々は、自分たちが海亀のように助言や慣習に逆らって上流に向かって泳いでいることに気づいた。彼らの技術的知識は高く評価されているが、党は彼らが忠誠心を分断するのではないかと恐れている。

　　習近平は、中国共産党中央委員会総書記で中国最高指導者である。2012年11月に総書記に就任し、国家主席となり、最高指導者の座に就いた。習近平の娘は、浙江大学に進学し外国語の同時通訳を学んだ。その後、アメリカのハーバード大学に入学し、４年間学んだ。卒業後、習近平の公務をサポートしている。習近平は、中国でしか教育を受けていない。

Reading

Many of China's top politicians were educated in the West. It did not endear them to it

endear ～ to …：～に…を愛させる

In the early 20th century thousands of Chinese Communist Party members went to Russia to learn how to stage a revolution and build a socialist state. The Russians, in turn, hoped the study programmes would give them lasting influence
5 over their Chinese comrades, many of whom would rise to positions of great power. But within a decade of becoming communist, China began squabbling with the Soviet Union. In 1961 leaders in Beijing denounced Soviet communism as the work of "revisionist traitors."

stage ～：～を実行する、起こす

squabbling with ～：～と争う

Beijing：中国政府

work of "revisionist traitors"：「修正主義者の裏切り者」の仕業

10 The episode holds sobering lessons for Western countries, which have hosted millions of Chinese students over the past four decades — many of whom have risen to positions of great power. While universities raked in cash, Western leaders hoped the experience would endear future Chinese leaders
15 to liberal values. But, as with the Russians, they have been disappointed. Today the party is more anti-Western than it has been in decades, a mood reflected in the words of President Xi Jinping and Qin Gang, the foreign minister, at a meeting of the National People's Congress this month.

President Xi Jinping：習近平国家主席

Qin Gang：秦剛

National People's Congress：全国人民代表会議

20 Foreign-educated students who return to China are known as *haigui* (sea turtles), a homophone for "returning home from abroad." For a long time those who entered China's bureaucracy found themselves swimming upstream. While their technical knowledge was valued, the party feared that
25 they might have divided loyalties. But as the number of *haigui* swelled, the distrust faded.

haigui：海亀

homophone：同音異義語

bureaucracy：官僚機構

loyalties：忠誠・支持

Today over 20% of Central Committee members — the 370 most powerful party officials in China — have had some foreign education, mostly at Western universities. Eight of
30 the 24 members of the Politburo have studied in Western countries, the most ever by far.

Central Committee：中央委員会

officials：幹部

Politburo：政治局

most ever by far：過去最多

Like many overseas Chinese students today, the leaders often focused on STEM subjects (science, technology, engineering and mathematics). A Politburo member called Chen Jining, who is the party boss of Shanghai, spent a decade in Britain studying engineering. Another member, Yuan Jiajun, studied at Germany's centre for aerospace research. He later ran the rocket programme that sent the first Chinese man into space.

But there was demand for other subjects, too. In 2002 Harvard University's Kennedy School of Government, working with Chinese institutions, set up a three-month programme to teach mid-ranking Chinese officials about administration. Similar short-term programmes sprang up at universities elsewhere in America and the West.

Despite all this, an anti-Western spirit permeates the leadership. Students in China's schools are warned not to be misled by foreign concepts. In February a teacher in Anhui province was denounced by a student for "worshipping the West and pandering to foreign powers" after he encouraged students to study abroad.

President Xi Jinping studied only in China. But his ideological tsar, Wang Huning, was a visiting scholar in America in 1988. He wrote a book about his experience which revealed admiration for some aspects of the country, such as the way presidents reliably leave office when their term ends. But, Mr Wang wrote, there were "undercurrents of crisis" caused by racial tensions, disintegrating families and poor education. For him, America mostly offered a lesson in what to avoid.

The Economist, March 9, 2023

Chen Jining：陳吉寧
party boss：党書記
Yuan Jiajun：袁家軍
centre for aerospace research：航空宇宙研究センター

Kennedy School of Government：ケネディ行政大学院

administration：行政（学）
sprang up：生まれた

permeates 〜：〜に浸透している

Anhui province：安徽省

pandering to 〜：〜に迎合する

tsar：権威
Wang Huning：王滬寧

term：任期
"undercurrents of crisis"：「危機の底流」
disintegrating families：家庭崩壊
in what to avoid：何を避けるべきかについての

Exercises

Multiple Choice

次の１～２の英文を完成させ、３～５の英文の質問に答えるために、ａ～ｄの中から最も適切なものを１つ選びなさい。

1. The writer states that Chinese Communist Party members used to go to Russia

   a. to develop their business skills.

   b. to study how to build socialism.

   c. to fight alongside Soviet soldiers against Western countries.

   d. to gain expertise in Russian language and culture.

2. Western leaders hoped Chinese studying overseas would

   a. explain the value of socialism to them.

   b. finish their studies quickly and focus on earning cash.

   c. come to see the value of liberal ideas.

   d. help to change Western educational methods.

3. Previously, what was Chinese bureaucrats' attitude to 'sea turtles'?

   a. They felt their technical knowledge was useless.

   b. They welcomed them enthusiastically.

   c. They wanted them to return overseas.

   d. They were suspicious of them.

4. What has been the impact of haigui on China's leadership?

   a. Their numbers have decreased.

   b. Their numbers have increased.

   c. They have helped China to trust the West more.

   d. They have popularized misleading foreign concepts.

5. What was Mr Wang's overall conclusion about America?

   a. It is well adapted to dealing with crises.

   b. Its political system is too unstable.

   c. Despite some positive aspects, its society is not a desirable model.

   d. It provides Chinese students with poor quality education.

True or False

本文の内容に合致するものに T （True）、合致しないものに F （False） をつけなさい。

(   ) **1.** Students who have studied abroad are known as sea turtles.

(   ) **2.** *Haigui*'s technical knowledge was once highly valued in China.

(   ) **3.** Chen Jining had long experience studying literature in Britain.

(   ) **4.** Students in China are welcoming Western liberalism.

(   ) **5.** Mr. Wang wrote that Americans enjoy an ideal society.

Vocabulary

次の 1 〜 7 は、「学ぶ」に関することわざです。（   ） 内に最も適切な下の a 〜 g の和文、また ［   ］ 内に下の①〜⑦の英文説明の中から 1 つずつ選び、記入しなさい。

1. There is no royal road to learning.   (   ) [   ]
2. Example is better than precept.   (   ) [   ]
3. Practice makes perfect.   (   ) [   ]
4. Seeing is believing.   (   ) [   ]
5. The pen is mightier than the sword.   (   ) [   ]
6. Where there's a will, there's a way.   (   ) [   ]
7. Work hard, play hard.   (   ) [   ]

a. 習うより慣れよ

b. よく学びよく遊べ

c. 百聞は一見にしかず

d. 学問に王道なし

e. 精神一到何事か成らざらん

f. 文は武よりも強し

g. 論より証拠

① If you try hard enough, you can do anything.

② Education is more powerful than physical force.

③ Hard work is the only way to succeed in your studies.

④ Don't believe anything without proof.

⑤ You not only study, but also play with your full effort.

⑥ Rather than tell people you should show them by your behavior.

⑦ Habit makes all things easy.

Unit 6

●バリ島　ロシアとウクライナからの避難民受け入れ
見直し

インドネシア・バリ島のエコビーチ風景。元々、欧米の観光客の人気スポットだったが、コロナ禍やロシアによるウクライナ侵攻で、ロシアやウクライナからの避難民だらけに
写真：NYIMAS LAULA／Redux／アフロ

Before you read

Bali Island　バリ島
インドネシア共和国バリ州に属する島

面積　5,682.86km²
人口　4,317,404人／**最大都市**　デンパサール
公用語　インドネシア語、バリ語／**宗教**　バリ・ヒンズー教

Russian Federation　ロシア連邦

面積　17,098,246km²（日本の約45倍）（世界1位）
首都・最大都市　モスクワ
公用語　ロシア語／**識字率**　99.7%
人口　145,872,000人（世界9位）
民族　スラブ人　82.7%／テュルク系　8.7%
　　　コーカサス系　3.7%／ウラル系　1.6%
宗教　ロシア正教会　63%／その他のキリスト教　4.5%
　　　イスラム教　6.6%／仏教　0.5%／ユダヤ教　0.6%
GDP　1兆6,572億米ドル（世界12位）
　　　1人当たりのGDP　11,289米ドル（世界65位）
通貨　ロシア・ルーブル／**政体**　共和制・連邦制

Ukraine　ウクライナ

ソビエト連邦より1991年8月24日独立

面積　603,700km²（日本の約1.6倍）（世界45位）
首都　キーウ
公用語　ウクライナ語／**識字率**　99.7%
人口　41,590,000人（南部クリミアを除く）
民族　ウクライナ人　77.8%／ロシア人　17.3%
　　　ベラルーシ人　0.6%／モルドバ人、クリミア人、ユダヤ人等
宗教　ウクライナ正教会　76.5%
　　　その他のキリスト教　4.4%／ユダヤ教　0.6%
GDP　1,555億ドル／1人当たりのGDP　3,726ドル
通貨　フリヴニャ／**政体**　共和制

次の1～5の語の説明として最も近いものをa～eから1つ選び、(　　)内に記入しなさい。

1. influencer　　(　　)
2. draft　　(　　)
3. vandalize　　(　　)
4. émigré　　(　　)
5. desecrate　　(　　)

a. person who left their own country
b. disrespect something sacred
c. damage property
d. person famous on social media
e. mandatory military service

Summary

次の英文は記事の要約です。下の語群から最も適切な語を1つ選び、(　　)内に記入しなさい。

1-32

The Balinese initially welcomed Russian and Ukrainian (　　　　　　) escaping the war. But too many Russians have been (　　　　　) local customs and religion. Some have even been (　　　　　) illegally. And both Russians and Ukrainians have been involved in motorbike (　　　　　). The island's governor now wants Indonesia's government to cancel their right to (　　　　　) on arrival.

accidents　　disrespecting　　tourists　　visas　　working

　ロシアがウクライナに侵略する中、軍の招集を逃れて、何千人ものロシア人とウクライナ人が2022年にインドネシアのバリ島にやってきた。最初は、砲撃から逃れてくるウクライナ人や徴兵を避けようとするロシア人を歓迎していた。さらに、33ドルで、即座に発給される30日間の観光ビザで入国が許可されていた。

　しかし、問題が起きている。あるロシア人は樹齢700年の聖なる木によじ登り、裸の姿を発信した。さらにロシア人ストリートアーティストが民家に勝手に反戦の壁画を描いた。ロシア人のティーンエージャーも学校を荒らして捕まった。ロシア人とウクライナ人がからんだバイクの事故も相次いでいる。交通違反は、ロシア人の56件に対し、インドネシア人は5件しか起こしていない。ロシア人の不法就労も明らかになっている。

　ロシア人の急増に地元州政府の対応が追いついていない。2022年は5万8000人ものロシア人が来島した。ウクライナ人は7000人だった。2023年1月だけで2万2500人ものロシア人がやってきた。バリ島のウクライナ人は、地元の経済に貢献し、税金をきちんと納め、いずれは帰ることを希望している。バリ島での不満の矛先の多くが、ロシア人に向けられているのは確かだろう。

Reading

1-33

A Refuge for Russians and Ukrainians, Bali Rethinks Its Open-Door Policy

For most of last year, thousands of Russians and Ukrainians flocked to the Indonesian island of Bali to escape the war. There they found refuge in a tropical paradise where locals rolled out the welcome mat for Ukrainians fleeing the shelling
5 and Russians dodging the draft.

Then, a Russian influencer scaled a 700-year-old sacred tree, naked.

After that, a Russian street artist painted an antiwar mural on a private house, and a Russian teenager was caught
10 vandalizing a school.

A string of recent motorbike collisions involving Russians and Ukrainians has raised questions about traffic safety on the island.

1-34

Now, the once-welcoming Balinese people have had
15 enough. Confronted with a barrage of complaints, the governor of Bali, Wayan Koster, announced earlier this month that he asked the Indonesian government to revoke Russia's and Ukraine's access to the country's visa-on-arrival program.

He said many of those who have flocked to Bali to avoid
20 the war have not only violated a number of local laws but have been seeking jobs while on short-term tourist visas.

The Balinese have long endured badly behaved tourists in mostly isolated incidents. Now, they complain regularly of half-naked foreigners riding motorbikes and desecrating
25 objects that are considered sacred on the predominantly Hindu island.

1-35

The Balinese were initially sympathetic to the plight of the new émigrés. Many extended credit for car and home rentals to Russians, who found themselves cut off from the international
30 payments system because of sanctions. After being sealed off for two years during the coronavirus pandemic, they were

Refuge：避難所	
flocked to ～：～に群がった	
fleeing the shelling：砲撃から逃れる	
dodging the draft：徴兵をかわす	
scaled ～：～をよじ登った	
sacred：聖なる	
naked：裸で	
mural：壁画	
vandalizing ～：～を破壊する	
collisions：衝突	
had enough：もう沢山だ	
Confronted with ～：～に直面した	
barrage of complaints：苦情の弾幕	
revoke ～：～を取り消す	
access to ～：～を入手する権利	
visa-on-arrival：到着ビザ	
badly behaved：行儀の悪い	
desecrating ～：～を冒瀆する	
Hindu：ヒンズー教徒の《インドネシアはイスラム教国だが、バリ島だけヒンズー教》	
plight：窮状	
émigrés：亡命者	
credit：信用取引	
payments system：決済システム	
sanctions：制裁	

eager for income.

But later, they discovered that many Russians had taken on jobs on the island — as surfing instructors and tour guides.
35 Some started their own car and home rental businesses, violating the laws governing tourist visas and taking away from local income.

1-36

Many Balinese say part of the issue is that the authorities are struggling to cope with the sudden influx of Russians,
40 who now make up the second-biggest group of tourists on the island after Australians. Last year, 58,000 Russians and 7,000 Ukrainians visited Bali. This January alone, 22,500 Russians arrived in the province.

In May 2022, the Indonesian government added Russia
45 and Ukraine to the list of countries eligible for its visa-on-arrival program.

1-37

Sandiaga Uno, the minister for tourism, indicated that the government was not going to revoke the visa program, as requested by the Bali governor. In a weekly address earlier
50 this month, he said that the number of people causing trouble was "not too significant." Last November, Mr. Sandiaga had told The New York Times that the government would help renew the tourist visas of those fleeing the war.

But the authorities in Bali have zeroed in on the rising
55 traffic violations involving Russians and Ukrainians that have sometimes turned deadly. In response, Mr. Wayan, the governor, announced last week a ban on all foreigners riding motorbikes, a decision that Mr. Sandiaga said should be reversed.

governing ～：～を管理する

issue：問題

cope with ～：～に対処する

influx：流入

countries eligible for ～：～の対象国

as requested：要請に応じて

address：会見

"not too significant"：「大きな影響を与えるほどではない」

zeroed in on ～：～に焦点を絞った

reversed：覆される

Sui-Lee Wee and Maktita Suhartono
The New York Times, March 24, 2023

Exercises

次の１〜３の英文の質問に答え、４〜５の英文を完成させるために、ａ〜ｄの中から最も
適切なものを１つ選びなさい。

1. What seems to be the main reason for more Russians and Ukrainians visiting Bali?

    a. To make anti-war protests.

    b. To find work.

    c. To escape the war.

    d. To rent homes and cars cheaply.

2. What measures does the governor have in mind?

    a. He wants to reduce the number of visitors from Russia and Ukraine.

    b. He plans to make Russians and Ukrainians wear shirts when riding.

    c. He is proposing a program whereby some tourists can work legally.

    d. He intends to ban non-Indonesian tourists from riding motorbikes.

3. On what do Sandiaga Uno and Wayan Koster disagree?

    a. The need to revoke access to visas-on-arrival.

    b. The necessity of banning tourists from riding bikes.

    c. The proportion of tourists who are troublemakers.

    d. All of the above.

4. Governor Wayan Koster asked the Indonesian government to revoke Russian and Ukrainian access to the visa-on-arrival program because

    a. too many were behaving disrespectfully or illegally.

    b. the two groups kept arguing with each other about the war.

    c. most of them had desecrated sacred sites.

    d. they did not observe rules to reduce Covid-19 infection.

5. Many Russian tourists face financial difficulties in Bali due to

    a. leaving their credit cards behind after fleeing in a hurry.

    b. the falling value of their currency since the war began.

    c. political policies restricting their access to Indonesia.

    d. economic sanctions blocking their use of international payment systems.

本文の内容に合致するものに T （True）、合致しないものに F （False）をつけなさい。

(   )   **1.** Many Russians and Ukrainians left for Indonesia to escape the war.

(   )   **2.** A Russian teenager destroyed school property.

(   )   **3.** Most Russians moved to Indonesia to work legally.

(   )   **4.** The Balinese still welcome Russians and Ukrainians warmly.

(   )   **5.** The Indonesian government started offering visa-on-arrival to Russians and Ukrainians in 2022.

Vocabulary

次の１～７は、移民や難民に関する英文です。下の語群から最も適切なものを１つ選び、（   ）内に記入しなさい。

1. An (   ) seeker wants protection and shelter in another country.

2. An Italian (   ) left Naples hoping to find work in Australia.

3. From the late 1970s, many (   ) people left Vietnam.

4. Japan has more economic migrants than human rights (   ).

5. (   ) have been forced to leave their country for various reasons.

6. On arrival you should present your passport to the (   ) officer.

7. Those birds (   ) north in summer and south in winter.

asylum	boat	emigrant	émigrés
immigration	migrate	refugees	

Unit **7**

●コロナウイルスの起源を巡る政治的闘い

中国武漢市にあるウイルス研究所内の P4研究棟風景。新型コロナウイルスの起源
を巡り、米中の政治的闘いの場となる。WHO（世界保健機関）の仕事は？

写真：AP ／アフロ

Before you read

Questions

1. What do you think the article will be about?

この記事は何の話題についてだと思いますか？

2. How can you travel in the middle of a pandemic?

パンデミック中に、どうやって旅行をしますか？

次の1〜5の語の説明として最も近いものをa〜eから1つ選び、（　　）内に記入しなさい。

1. stonewall　　（　　）　　**a.** refuse to cooperate

2. incomplete　（　　）　　**b.** advocate trying to influence policymakers

3. lobbyist　　（　　）　　**c.** succeed

4. leak　　　　（　　）　　**d.** something emerging by accident

5. prevail　　　（　　）　　**e.** lacking or unfinished

　次の英文は記事の要約です。下の語群から最も適切な語を1つ選び、（　）内に記入しなさい。

1-38

　　The scientifically (　　　　　) hunt for Covid-19's origins has been complicated in America by partisan politics. Many Republicans are fixated on the idea of a lab (　　　　　), which some Democrats view as an effort to (　　　　　) from President Trump's failings. Although (　　　　　) transmission at a market seems more likely, Republicans are again pushing lab leak theories after (　　　　　) control of the House.

> animal　　crucial　　distract　　leak　　regaining

　2023年5月8日にコロナが5類に移行し、季節性インフルエンザと同等の扱いになる。新型コロナウイルス感染症の流行も4年目となった。新型コロナウイルスは2019年12月に中国の武漢市で発生し、武漢から世界に広がっていったと言われている。武漢で流行が認知された当初は海鮮市場に関連する症例が多かったということで、ここで売られていた野生動物あるいはタヌキが感染源であり、そこからヒトに感染するようになったのではないかという推測もあった。しかし、この海鮮市場とは全く関連がない症例が2019年12月上旬の時点で複数報告されており、この海鮮市場が新型コロナウイルスの起源ではない可能性も指摘されている。

　ヨーロッパでは2019年12月の時点で新型コロナウイルスが見つかっている。イタリアでは、2019年12月にミラノとトリノから収集された排水から新型コロナウイルスが検出されたと発表されている。また、フランスでも同時期に新型コロナウイルスが検出されたという症例報告が出ている。日本で最初に新型コロナ感染者が報告されたのは1月6日に武漢市から日本に帰国した患者だった。新型コロナウイルス感染症の流行も4年目に入り、武漢ウイルス研究所から漏れたのではないかという説が強力とされる。

1-39

Lab Leak or Not? How Politics Shaped the Battle Over Covid's Origin

WASHINGTON — The story of the hunt for Covid's origin is partly about the stonewalling by China that has left scientists with incomplete evidence, all of it about a virus that is constantly changing. For all the data suggesting that the
5 virus may have jumped into people from wild animals at a Chinese market, conclusive proof remains out of reach, as it does for the competing hypothesis that the virus leaked from a lab.

But the story is also about politics and how both Democrats
10 and Republicans have filtered the available evidence through their partisan lenses.

1-40

Some Republicans grew fixated on the idea of a lab leak after former President Donald J. Trump raised it in the early months of the pandemic despite scant evidence supporting
15 it. That turned the theory toxic for many Democrats, who viewed it as an effort by Mr. Trump to distract from his administration's failings in containing the spread of the virus.

The intense political debate, now in its fourth year, has at times turned scientists into lobbyists, competing for
20 policymakers' time and favor.

1-41

Even as the idea of an accidental lab leak has now gained standing in Washington, findings reported last week bolstered the market theory. Mining a trove of genetic data taken from swabs at the Huanan Seafood Wholesale Market in Wuhan in
25 early 2020, virus experts said they found samples containing genetic material from both the coronavirus and illegally traded raccoon dogs.

The new data from the market suggests that China is holding onto clues that could reshape the debate. But for now,
30 at least, the idea of a lab leak seems to have prevailed in the court of public opinion: Two recent polls show that roughly

Lab Leak：研究所からの漏洩	
stonewalling：妨害	
remains out of reach：まだ到達していない	
as 〜：〜と同様に	
hypothesis：仮説	
Democrats：米民主党	
Republicans：米共和党	
partisan：党派の	
toxic：ストレスばかり溜まるような	
distract from 〜：〜から気をそらす	
competing for 〜：〜を奪い合う	
favor：支持	
gained standing：支持を得た	
findings：調査結果	
Mining 〜：〜を検索する	
genetic：遺伝学上の	
raccoon dogs：タヌキ	
polls：世論調査	

two-thirds of Americans believe that Covid probably started in a lab.

At the end of April 2020, Mr. Trump announced that he had seen intelligence that supported a lab leak but was "not allowed" to share it.

Democrats showed little inclination to investigate the pandemic's origins. Like the president's references to the "China virus," his suggestion of a lab leak sounded to them like xenophobia and risked fueling anti-Asian sentiment.

When Mr. Biden won the 2020 election, some experts who called for a fuller investigation of the lab leak hypothesis saw an opportunity to persuade Democrats to give the idea a closer look.

New information about the work of the Wuhan Institute of Virology was also intensifying concerns about a lab leak, even as hard evidence of such an incident remained elusive.

In the Senate, aides were many months into a bipartisan investigation of the origins of the pandemic, including the lab leak idea. The resulting report — in a sign of enduring partisan divisions, it was endorsed only by Republicans — said that safety risks at the Wuhan Institute of Virology made a lab leak likely. Weeks after the report's release, Republicans won control of the House.

This month, the new House Subcommittee on the Coronavirus Pandemic convened its first hearing to examine the pandemic's origins. The market theory was barely discussed.

Sheryl Gay Stolberg and Benjamin Mueller
The New York Times, March 19, 2023

xenophobia：外国人嫌悪

called for ～：～を求めた

persuade ～ to …：～に…するよう説得する

Wuhan Institute of Virology：武漢ウイルス学研究所

intensifying ～：～を強めている

concerns：懸念

hard：確固とした

elusive：捉え難い

Senate：米上院

aides：補佐官たち

were many months into ～：～に何か月もかけていた

endorsed：支持された

likely：発生しやすい、可能性が高い

House：米下院

Subcommittee on ～：～に関する小委員会

convened ～：～を召集した

Exercises

Multiple Choice

次の1～2の英文の質問に答え、3～5の英文を完成させるために、a～dの中から最も適切なものを1つ選びなさい。

1. What is the main focus of this article?

    a. The political nature of U.S. debates about the origins of Covid-19.

    b. The way politics has influenced science in China.

    c. The analysis of genetic material from raccoon dogs.

    d. The spread of the virus around America.

2. What does the writer appear to think about the origins of the virus?

    a. The lab leak theory is ridiculous and not worth investigating.

    b. Transmission at a market seems more likely than at a lab.

    c. The virus definitely came from racoon dogs.

    d. We will never know where the virus came from.

3. Many Democrats view the lab leak theory negatively because

    a. it created xenophobia in China.

    b. data from the Huanan Seafood Wholesale Market was unreliable.

    c. it was promoted by Trump for political reasons.

    d. the theory has barely been discussed.

4. According to recent polls, the idea that Covid originated in a lab

    a. is supported only by Democrats.

    b. is supported only by Republicans.

    c. is rejected by a majority of Americans.

    d. is believed by a majority of Americans.

5. The Senate report concluded that a lab leak was likely because

    a. the Democrats stopped criticizing Trump after Biden's election.

    b. new details about racoon dogs in the Wuhan market had emerged.

    c. it found evidence of safety risks at the Institute of Virology.

    d. its report came out after the Republicans gained control of the House.

本文の内容に合致するものにＴ（True）、合致しないものにＦ（False）をつけなさい。

(   ) **1.** The American Democrats and Republicans debated about the origins of Covid-19.

(   ) **2.** Only Republicans believe Covid-19 originated in a lab.

(   ) **3.** Many Democrats consider the lab leak theory negatively.

(   ) **4.** The idea of a lab leak seemed to be promoted by Trump for political reasons.

(   ) **5.** Mr. Biden called the Covid-19 the "China virus."

Vocabulary

次の１〜７は、「Coronavirus」に関する英文です。日本文に合わせて、適当な語を下の語群から１つ選び、（   ）内に記入しなさい。

1. 特に不要不急の仕事の場合は、できるだけ在宅勤務をお願いしていました。
The authorities asked people to work from home as much as possible, especially if their work was considered (   ) and nonurgent.

2. 政府は、海外への渡航の自粛をお願いしていました。
The government had asked people here to refrain from travel (   ).

3. 自粛ムードは、経済にも影響していた。
The air of (   ) had also had an effect on the economy.

4. 感染拡大で日経平均株価が下落した。
The Nikkei Stock Average went down as the (   ) of contagion rose.

5. ２回ワクチン接種を受けた人は、今回で３回目の接種となります。
People who have been vaccinated twice can now get a (   ).

6. マスクの着用は、個人の判断となりました。
(   ) a mask is a personal decision.

7. コロナが５類に移行し、インフルエンザと同等の扱いになります。
Moving to type 5, Corona is being treated the (   ) as influenza.

booster	nonessential	overseas	same
self-restraint	spread	wearing	

Unit 8

●AUKUS の潜水艦に関する協定は地域集団安全保障の柱

米英豪首脳会談で豪への原子力潜水艦配備計画を発表。対中国包囲計画が着々と進む

写真：AFP／アフロ

Before you read

Commonwealth of Australia
オーストラリア連邦

英連邦王国の一国

面積　7,692,024km²（日本の約20倍）（世界6位）
人口　25,364,000人（世界55位）
民族　ヨーロッパ系　80%／アジア系　12%／アボリジニ　2%
首都　キャンベラ／最大都市　シドニー
公用語　英語／識字率　99%
宗教　キリスト教　64%（カトリック　25.8%　聖公会　18.7%）
　　　非キリスト教　5%　無宗教　18.7%
政体　立憲君主制
GDP　1兆3,800億米ドル（世界14位）
　　　1人当たり GDP　55,000米ドル（世界15位）
通貨　オーストラリア（豪）・ドル

the United Kingdom of Great Britain and Northern Ireland
英国（グレートブリテン及びアイルランド連合王国）

面積　244,820km²（日本の本州と四国とほぼ同じ）（世界78位）
人口　67,530,000人（世界21位）／識字率　99%
公用語　英語／首都　ロンドン
民族　イングランド人　5,500万人／スコットランド人　540万人
　　　（北）アイルランド人181万人／ウエールズ人　300万人
宗教　キリスト教　71.6%／イスラム教徒　2.7%／ヒンズー教　1.0%
GDP　2兆8,288億ドル（世界5位）／通貨　UKポンド
　　　1人当たり GDP　42,580ドル（世界22位）
政体　立憲君主制

次の１～５の語の説明として最も近いものをａ～ｅから１つ選び、（　）内に記入しなさい。

1. unveil   (　　)   **a.** anger
2. check   (　　)   **b.** change
3. fury   (　　)   **c.** estimated or anticipated
4. projected   (　　)   **d.** block or counter
5. amend   (　　)   **e.** reveal

Summary

次の英文は記事の要約です。下の語群から最も適切な語を１つ選び、（　）内に記入しなさい。

1-44

Under the new AUKUS alliance, Australia, the U.K., and the U.S. have (　　　　) plans to build a new (　　　　) of nuclear-powered submarines. This has (　　　　) Beijing, which has been expanding its influence in the Indo-Pacific. Perhaps this (　　　　) of the "Anglosphere" in the Far East should be (　　　　) with the involvement of other allies such as Japan.

> fleet   infuriated   moderated   reassertion   unveiled

> AUKUS オーカスは、Australia オーストラリア・United Kingdom イギリス・United States アメリカの頭文字をとり、アメリカ、イギリスおよびオーストラリアの三国間の軍事同盟である。2021年９月15日にこの同盟が発足した。アメリカとイギリスは、オーストラリアによる原子力潜水艦の開発および配備を支援し、太平洋地域における西側諸国の軍事影響力を強化することを目指している。共同声明では、特定の国名は挙げられていないが、インド太平洋地域において影響力を増す中国に対抗する意図があると述べている。
> この軍事同盟の協定は、潜水艦や自律型無人潜水機、長距離攻撃能力、敵基地攻撃能力などの軍事分野やサイバー戦争の抑止のためのサイバーセキュリティ、AI、また量子コンピュータを用いた暗号化技術の最先端テクノロジーの開発を主要な対象としている。また、アメリカとイギリスは、核弾頭を搭載した弾道ミサイルなどを含む核兵器インフラストラクチャーに関するコンポーネントも含まれ、軍事面に焦点を合わせている。

Reading

1-45

AUKUS sub deal is one pillar of regional security

The outlines of the Australia-U.K.-U.S. security partnership became clearer this week as the three countries unveiled plans to develop a new fleet of nuclear-powered attack submarines.

The ambitious project is designed to help check China's
5 growing power in the Indo-Pacific and has, as a result, triggered Beijing's fury.

AUKUS was announced in 2021 as an "enhanced trilateral security partnership." Its birth was controversial, starting with the renunciation of a deal with France to provide the next
10 generation of Australian submarines. That project was behind schedule and Canberra jumped at the opportunity to acquire nuclear-powered subs, which travel farther, stay underwater longer and are quieter than the diesel model that Paris was building.

1-46
15 In stage one, U.S. submarines will make regular port calls in Australia while Australian officers are trained on how to operate nuclear-powered boats. In stage two, around 2027, as many as five U.S. and British subs will be forward deployed to Western Australia. In stage three, in the early 2030s, Australia
20 will buy three Virginia-class submarines and have the option to purchase two more.

Meanwhile, the three countries will develop a new submarine class that will be based on a British design, will use cutting-edge U.S. technology and will be built in Australia and
25 Britain. One sub will be built every two years from the late 2030s to the late 2050s, eight of which will be constructed in Australia. The 20,000 jobs projected to be created in Australia are a sweetener for that country.

1-47
Realizing the potential of AUKUS will not be easy.
30 First, there is Australia's capacity for such a huge project. It will require "a whole of nation" effort, said Australian Prime Minister Anthony Albanese, who added that AUKUS

AUKUS：インド太平洋地域安全保障協定

sub deal：潜水艦に関する協定

unveiled 〜：〜を発表した

fleet：艦隊

nuclear-powered attack submarines：攻撃型原子力潜水艦

check 〜：〜を阻止する

fury：怒り

trilateral：三国間の

renunciation：破棄

Canberra：キャンベラ《この場合オーストラリア政府》

port calls：寄港

officers：将校

as many as 〜：〜もの

forward deployed to 〜：〜に前方展開される

projected to 〜：〜と予測される

capacity for 〜：〜に対する能力

"represents the biggest single investment in Australia's defense capability in all of our history," with the total cost reckoned to be at 368 billion Australian dollars ($245 billion) over the next three decades.

Then there is China's opposition. Beijing flatly rejects the AUKUS governments' argument that the project targets no single country and is instead intended to promote regional security. A Chinese Foreign Ministry spokesperson warned that the initiative is "an outdated Cold War zero-sum mentality," adding that "it will only exacerbate an arms race … and hurt regional peace and stability."

A third possible obstacle are U.S. rules that inhibit the transfer of advanced technologies. Remarkably for a deal that the U.S. has been instrumental in creating and argues is crucial to regional peace and stability, its own regulations have to be amended for it to proceed.

One criticism of AUKUS deserves attention: the charge that it represents the reassertion of "the Anglosphere." There is something anomalous about an alliance of just those three nations in this part of the world. They would do well to consider the addition of other partners, both to share the fruits of the deal, especially the technologies, and to soften its image. AUKUS can be a bulwark of regional security but it will be even more effective with additional partners, Japan among them.

The Japan Times, March 17, 2023.

reckoned to ~：~と考えられる

argument：主張

initiative：新たな取り組み

Cold War：米ソ冷戦時代の《第2次世界大戦後の東西両陣営間の緊張状態》

zero-sum：ゼロ・サム《負け分、勝ち分の和がゼロになる》

exacerbate ~：~を悪化させる

arms race：軍拡競争

obstacle are U.S. rules：《rules が主語》

inhibit ~：~を禁止する

argues：《主語は U.S.》

is：《主語は deal》

amended：修正される

criticism of ~：~に対する批判

deserves ~：~に値する

charge：非難

reassertion：再主張

"the Anglosphere"：「英語圏」

anomalous：異常な

alliance：同盟

would do well to ~：~すれば良いだろう

bulwark：防波堤

Exercises

Multiple Choice

次の、1〜2の英文を完成させ、3〜5の英文の質問に答えるために、a〜dの中から最も適切なものを1つ選びなさい。

1. The main purpose of the Australia-U.K.-U.S. security partnership is

    a. to enhance regional trade relations.

    b. to promote global disarmament.

    c. to counter China's growing power.

    d. to address climate change issues.

2. China views the AUKUS project as

    a. a step towards ending the arms race.

    b. a threat to itself and to regional stability.

    c. an opportunity to increase its military exports.

    d. a positive development for global security.

3. Why did Australia decide to acquire nuclear-powered submarines?

    a. They were cheaper than those offered by France.

    b. France was behind schedule in supplying diesel submarines.

    c. Australia wanted to strengthen its nuclear power capacity.

    d. China pressured Australia to acquire nuclear-powered submarines.

4. What might hinder the implementation of the AUKUS project?

    a. Lack of political support from Australia.

    b. Financial instability in the U.K.

    c. Opposition from France.

    d. U.S. restrictions on technology transfer.

5. How does the author suggest AUKUS could be more effective?

    a. By reducing its huge budget.

    b. By strengthening ties with China.

    c. By including additional regional partners.

    d. By focusing more on technology.

True or False

本文の内容に合致するものにT（True）、合致しないものにF（False）をつけなさい。

(　　) **1.** The goal of AUKUS is to support China's power in the Indo-Pacific.

(　　) **2.** AUKUS is a bilateral security partnership.

(　　) **3.** Australia has an opportunity to acquire nuclear-powered submarines.

(　　) **4.** The nuclear-powered submarines bound for Australia can travel farther but cannot stay underwater as long as the diesel models France offered.

(　　) **5.** The writer suggests Japan could be involved in the AUKUS partnership.

Vocabulary

次のクロスワードパズルの Across 横、Down 縦の英文説明を読み、Unit 8 の記事から最も適切な語句を見つけ、□の中に1文字ずつ入れなさい。

Clues across

3. buy
6. irregular
9. stop or block
10. worsen

Clues down

1. defense
2. large island nation
4. agreement
5. ten years
7. underwater vehicle
8. safety

●スコットランドでイスラム教徒の首相誕生

英国の政治的多様性

スコットランド自治政府首相にイスラム教徒が就任し、英国の政治的多様性が明らかに

写真：代表撮影／ロイター／アフロ

Before you read

United Kingdam
of Great Britain and
Northern Ireland

Belfast
Northern
Ireland
Scotland
Glasgow
Edinburgh
Liverpool
Dublin◎
Leeds
Birmingham
Ireland
Wales
England
Cardiff
London
◎
Bristol

Scotland　スコットランド

英国（グレートブリテン及び北アイルランド連合王国）を構成する国の１つ。グレートブリテン島の北３分の１を占める。1707年５月に英国の一部になった。

面積　77,910km²
人口　5,254,800人
公用語　英語、スコットランド・ゲール語
首都　エジンバラ
宗教　スコットランド国教会　42.4%／カトリック　16%
　　　イスラム教　0.8%／ヒンズー教　0.1%
　　　ユダヤ教　0.1%
通貨　UK ポンド
政体　立憲君主制　1999年スコットランド議会が再設置され、国内政策の多くの分野で権限を持っている。首長は、首相である。

次の１～５の語の説明として最も近いものをa～eから１つ選び、（　　）内に記入しなさい。

1.	diversification	（　　）	**a.**	unfriendliness or opposition
2.	expectation	（　　）	**b.**	becoming more varied
3.	autonomous	（　　）	**c.**	prejudice against a different ethnicity
4.	racism	（　　）	**d.**	assumption
5.	hostility	（　　）	**e.**	self-governing

次の英文は記事の要約です。下の語群から最も適切な語を１つ選び、（　　）内に記入しなさい。

1-50

Humza Yousaf has become the first person of (　　　　　　) to lead the Scottish government and the first Muslim leader of a Western (　　　　　　). His appointment reflects the (　　　　　　) of U.K. politics. 10% of (　　　　　　), including the prime minister, foreign secretary, home secretary and trade secretary, are people of color. (　　　　　　) Ireland also has a leader with an Indian background.

color　　democracy　　diversification　　neighboring　　parliamentarians

Humza Haroon Yousaf フムザ・ハルーン・ユサフは、1985年４月７日生まれの38歳である。スコットランドの政治家であり、2023年３月からスコットランド国民党 SNP の首相である。グラスゴーでパキスタン移民の子として生まれたユサフは、グラスゴー大学で政治を学び、2007年にスコットランド議会に選出された最初のイスラム教徒である。

ユサフは、2018年法務長官として入閣し、ヘイトクライム法案を提出した。2021年、彼は COVID-19パンデミックの後期段階で保健長官に任命され、NHS の回復とワクチン接種プログラムの大量展開を担当した。2023年の SNP 党首選挙で勝利し、ケイト・フォーブスを52％対48％で破り、初代大臣に任命され、最年少、初のスコットランド系アジア人、初のイスラム教徒として就任した。ユサフの政策は、言論の自由と表現の自由の権利を維持しながら、既存の法律を簡素化し、迫害されたマイノリティをさらに保護すると約束した。さらに、スコットランドの政府高官の間で人種の多様性を高めることへの支持を表明し、「すべての人の平等に固くコミットしている」と述べ、同性結婚とトランスジェンダーの人々のジェンダー改革を支持してきた。

Reading

1-51

Muslim leader for Scotland a sign of U.K. political diversity

Muslim：イスラム教徒の

LONDON (AP) — Humza Yousaf was confirmed as first minister of Scotland on Tuesday, becoming the first person of color to head the Scottish government, and the first Muslim national leader in any Western democracy.

AP：《記事配信元の通信社名》
first minister：首相
person of color：有色人種
head 〜：〜を率いる

5　The milestone comes five months after the U.K. got its first Hindu leader in Prime Minister Rishi Sunak. Britain's capital city is headed by London Mayor Sadiq Khan, the son of Pakistani immigrants.

milestone：画期的な出来事

All three politicians reflect the accelerating diversification
10　of politics in Britain, a country whose imperialist past has — uncertainly and sometimes painfully — forged a multiethnic present.

imperialist past：帝国主義の過去
forged 〜：〜を築き上げた
multiethnic：多民族の

1-52

"There's an expectation now, or a familiarity with diversity in British politics, that we don't see in other European
15　countries," said Sunder Katwala of British Future, a think-tank that studies identity and race.

expectation：期待
familiarity：慣れ親しみ

Lawmakers in the Edinburgh-based Scottish parliament voted on Tuesday to confirm 37-year-old Yousaf as first minister, a day after he was elected leader of the governing
20　Scottish National Party. Scotland, a country of 5.5 million people, is part of the United Kingdom, but has a semi-autonomous government with broad power in areas including health and education.

Lawmakers：議員
governing：与党の
Scottish National Party：スコットランド国民党
semi-autonomous：半自治の
with broad power：幅広い権限を持つ

1-53

In an acceptance speech Monday, Yousaf said he was
25　"forever thankful that my grandparents made the trip from the Punjab to Scotland over 60 years ago."

acceptance：受諾
Punjab：パンジャブ《インド北西部からパキスタンに及ぶ一地方》

"As immigrants to this country, who knew barely a word of English, they could not have imagined their grandson would one day be on the cusp of being the next first minister
30　of Scotland," he said. "From the Punjab to our parliament, this is a journey over generations that reminds us that we should

on the cusp of 〜：〜の最前線で
reminds 〜 …：〜に…のことを思い出させる

celebrate migrants who contribute so much to our country."

The U.K. has not always heeded that reminder: migrants have often experienced racism and hostility both covert and overt. That hostility remains government policy for people who arrived by unauthorized means: Sunak's government plans to detain and deport anyone who crosses the English Channel in small boats, and wants to send some asylum-seekers on a one-way trip to Rwanda.

But British society and politics have grown markedly more diverse. About 18% of the population is non-white, and many people have roots in countries the British Empire once ruled, including India, Pakistan and Caribbean nations such as Jamaica.

Yousaf joined the pro-independence SNP in 2005, inspired partly by its then-leader Alex Salmond's opposition to the U.S.-led invasion of Iraq, which the U.K. under Prime Minister Tony Blair had joined. Yousaf said he felt independence from the U.K. was the only way to ensure Scotland would not become embroiled in another illegal war.

Britain is not the only European country whose politics are growing more diverse. Irish Prime Minister Leo Varadkar has an Indian father, and Portuguese leader Antonio Costa also has South Asian roots.

But Britain has seen rapid political change. Forty years ago there were no ethnic-minority lawmakers in the British Parliament. Now there are 65 — making up 10% of the total. The foreign secretary, home secretary and trade secretary in Sunak's government are all people of color.

Jill Lawless
AP News / The Toronto Star, March 28, 2023.

---

heeded 〜：〜に注意を払った

reminder：注意事項

covert and overt：秘かに及びあからさまに

unauthorized：無許可の

detain 〜：〜を勾留する

deport 〜：〜を強制送還する

asylum-seekers：亡命希望者

Rwanda：（第３国の）ルワンダ《アフリカ中部の共和国》

inspired：触発されて

ensure 〜：〜を確実にする

embroiled in 〜：〜に巻き込まれる

seen 〜：〜を経験した

ethnic-minority：少数民族の

foreign secretary：外務大臣《secretary は米国では長官》

home secretary：内務大臣

trade secretary：商務大臣

Exercises

Multiple Choice

次の1～2の英文を完成させ、3～5の英文の質問に答えるために、a～dの中から最も適切なものを1つ選びなさい。

1. Humza Yousaf was inspired to join the SNP by

    a. Alex Salmond's attitude to the invasion of Iraq.

    b. Rishi Sunak's policies on economic reform.

    c. Sadiq Khan's election as mayor of London.

    d. Leo Varadkar's appointment as prime minister of Ireland.

2. In the last 40 years ethnic-minority members of the U.K. Parliament

    a. have increased from zero to 65.

    b. have increased from ten to 65.

    c. have gone up by 65%.

    d. have gone from 10% to 65%.

3. Who is the U.K.'s first Hindu Prime Minister?

    a. Humza Yousaf.

    b. Rishi Sunak.

    c. Sadiq Khan.

    d. Leo Varadkar.

4. What do the Mayor of London and the U.K. foreign secretary have in common?

    a. Their parents come from Scotland.

    b. They are both in Rishi Sunak's cabinet.

    c. They are both people of color.

    d. They are both members of the SNP.

5. What proportion of Britain's population is non-white?

    a. Under 8%.

    b. Nearly 10%.

    c. Almost 20%.

    d. Over 20%.

本文の内容に合致するものにＴ（True）、合致しないものにＦ（False）をつけなさい。

(   ) **1.** Non-white members of the U.K. parliament have increased a lot recently.

(   ) **2.** Rishi Sunak is the U.K.'s first Muslim Prime Minister.

(   ) **3.** Humza Yousaf is Scotland's first Muslim leader.

(   ) **4.** Sadiq Khan is the son of Indian immigrants.

(   ) **5.** The U.K.'s society and politics have become more diverse.

Vocabulary

次の１～８は、スコットランドの都市・文化・習慣・食物に関する語句です。下のａ～ｈ の説明文の中から最も適切なものを１つ選び、（   ）内に記入しなさい。

1. Edinburgh   (   )

2. Glasgow   (   )

3. Haggis   (   )

4. International Festival   (   )

5. Loch Ness   (   )

6. Saint Andrew   (   )

7. Scotch whisky   (   )

8. Tartan kilt   (   )

a. the national saint of Scotland

b. a city and port in Western Scotland on the River Clyde

c. a large and very deep lake in Northern Scotland

d. a skirt worn by Scotsmen with many pressed folds at the back and sides

e. a food made from the heart and other organs of a sheep and boiled inside a skin made from the sheep's stomach

f. the capital of Scotland, in the east of the country on the River Forth

g. a yearly program of musical and theatrical events taking place in Edinburgh

h. strong alcoholic drink made from malted grain like barley, produced in Scotland

●アニメに救われ、イタリア人が日本で精神科医に

東京都秋葉原駅近くの中央通りは今や「アニメ・ストリート」
と化す
写真：アフロ

Before you read

Italian Republic
イタリア共和国

面積　302,000km²（日本の約5分の4）
人口　60,368,000人
首都　ローマ
公用語　イタリア語
宗教　カトリック　79％／プロテスタント　1％
　　　無宗教　11％
識字率　99.3％
政体　共和制
GDP　2兆1,013億ドル
　　　1人当たりのGDP　35,473ドル（世界23位）
通貨　ユーロ

次の1～5の語句の説明として最も近いものをa～eから1つ選び、（　）内に記入しなさい。

1. nobility　　　　（　　）　　**a.** disturbed by a bad experience
2. recluse　　　　（　　）　　**b.** close or deep
3. intimate　　　　（　　）　　**c.** someone living in isolation
4. traumatized　　（　　）　　**d.** doctor specializing in mental disorders
5. psychiatrist　　（　　）　　**e.** high moral qualities

Summary

　次の英文は記事の要約です。下の語群から最も適切な語を1つ選び、（　）内に記入しなさい。

1-56　　An Italian (　　　　　　) working in Tokyo hopes to highlight anime as a way of encouraging people to seek (　　　　　　) for mental issues. A lonely child, Dr. Panto found (　　　　　) in anime and Japanese culture. Through (　　　　　) he passed the Japanese Language Aptitude Test in record time. He then moved to Japan to study under a leading researcher on *hikikomori* (　　　　　).

inspiration　　psychiatrist　　recluses　　self-study　　treatment

　　イタリア人精神科医パントー・フランチェスコ32歳。子供の頃から日本のアニメやゲームに励まされ、日本で働くことを選んだ。ひきこもり問題を研究し、心の不調を抱える多くの患者を日々診療している。「日本人は自分の悩みを人に相談したりせずに、抱え込んでしまう傾向がある」と語っている彼は、シチリア出身のイタリア人である。ローマの名門大学の医学部を終え、7年前に来日。筑波大学の医学部で学んだ後、日本の医師免許を取得し、現在、慶應義塾大学病院や複数のクリニックで診察にあたっている。
　　フランチェスコが日本で精神科医になることを目指したのは、幼い頃の趣味や体験にあった。小さい頃から同世代の男子と共通の話題をあまり持てず、日本のアニメに興味を抱いた。仲間はずれになったり、いじめにあったり、また高校の頃には、ひきこもりに近い状態になったこともある。そんなときに気持ちを支えてくれたのが、日本のアニメやゲームだった。好きなキャラクターに自分を投影して、そのキャラクター目線で現実の問題を見つめ直すと、あたかも自分の問題を鑑賞するような形で悩みに向き合えるようになった。日本文化が持つ芸術的で、美的な部分に感動し、一方、社会の混沌とした状態にも好奇心が湧いてきた。彼自身にもひきこもり的なところがあったから感情移入もできた。

1-57

Italian, saved by anime, becomes psychiatrist in Japan

psychiatrist：精神科医

It all started when Panto was 10 years old and glued to the TV screen showing the Italian version of the "Pretty Guardian Sailor Moon" anime series.

glued to ～：～に釘付けになる

"Pretty Guardian Sailor Moon"：『美少女戦士セーラームーン』

At the time, "Dragon Ball," another TV anime series from
5 Japan featuring a hero who becomes stronger as he defeats his enemies, was popular among Italian boys. But Panto was more attracted to the nobility and beauty of the girl characters in "Sailor Moon," "Magic Knight Rayearth," "Miracle Girls" and other shows.

"Dragon Ball"：『ドラゴンボール』

featuring ～：～を描く

attracted to ～：～に惹かれた

nobility：気高さ

"Magic Knight Rayearth"：『魔法騎士レイアース』

"Miracle Girls"：『ミラクルガールズ』

1-58

10 Around that time, he watched a TV program about Japan. The show introduced beautiful landscapes and traditional culture from across the country. It also covered social issues, such as "hikikomori" recluses.

Unable to find a place in Italy where he belonged, Panto
15 identified himself with recluses in Japan and felt an intimate connection with the country.

identified ～ with…：～と…を同一視した

As he found himself through anime, he became eager to learn about the human mind and body, as well as the secrets of life. Panto studied hard and entered medical school at a
20 university in Rome.

medical school：医学部

1-59

As a second-year med student, he came across a life-changing anime. "Neon Genesis Evangelion" featured traumatized characters suffering from various complexes. Panto was shocked by the anime's profound story and
25 the complicated portrayals of feelings experienced by the characters.

came across ～：～と出会った

"Neon Genesis Evangelion"：『新世紀エヴァンゲリオン』

traumatized：トラウマを抱えた

suffering from ～：～に苦しむ

portrayals of feelings：感情描写

He previously had a vague desire to visit Japan, but he developed a concrete travel plan after watching the anime.

concrete：具体的な

Panto could not afford Japanese language classes, so
30 he learned an entire kanji dictionary by rote to improve his proficiency. He memorized all 4,000 kanji characters in the

learned ～ by rote：～を暗記した

proficiency：習熟度

dictionary in just three months. But the most useful study material for him was "Detective Conan." He watched the anime show over and over and transcribed all dialogue.

After learning Japanese on his own for about one year and three months, he took the Japanese Language Aptitude Test for non-native speakers. Panto passed the exam on his first attempt, although even native speakers have difficulties scoring full marks on the N1 test.

40 He came to Japan in 2015 under a scholarship program offered by the Japanese education ministry and studied under Tamaki Saito, a professor at the University of Tsukuba who is a leading figure in research on hikikomori.

Panto had already obtained an EU medical license, but 45 he had to pass the national exam for medical practitioners to work as a physician in Japan.

Panto currently works at several clinics in the Tokyo metropolitan area. He is concerned that mental health problems tend to be neglected in Japan.

50 "Hikikomori issues have become a social phenomenon, and the suicide rate is particularly high here compared with other developed countries," he said, adding that Japanese people feel strongly uncomfortable about seeing a psychiatrist.

"Japanese anime is complicated and profound. I think 55 there are people who can be helped with the power of its storytelling," Panto said. "I think we can make them feel less hesitant about seeing a doctor if they can receive treatment while they enjoy anime."

Erina Ito
The Asahi Shimbun Asia & Japan Watch, April 29, 2023

"Detective Conan"：『名探偵コナン』

transcribed all dialogue：全セリフを書き起こした

learning 〜 on his own：〜を独学で学習する

Japanese Language Aptitude Test：日本語能力試験

N1：認定レベル１（１級）

education ministry：文部科学省

studied under Tamaki Saito：斉藤環に師事した

leading figure：第一人者

EU：欧州連合

neglected：軽視される

phenomenon：現象

suicide rate：自殺率

uncomfortable：違和感

seeing 〜：〜を受診する

Exercises

次の１〜５の英文の質問に答えるために、ａ〜ｄの中から最も適切なものを１つ選びなさい。

1. What initially attracted Panto to Japanese anime?

   a. Their popularity with other Italian boys.
   b. Noble and beautiful female characters.
   c. Their portrayal of social issues.
   d. The hero in *Dragon Ball*.

2. Which anime had a life-changing impact on Panto in his second year of med school?

   a. *Pretty Guardian Sailor Moon*.
   b. *Magic Knight Rayearth*.
   c. *Miracle Girls*.
   d. *Neon Genesis Evangelion*.

3. How did Panto start learning Japanese?

   a. By joining a language class.
   b. By memorizing a kanji dictionary.
   c. By translating *Detective Conan* into Italian.
   d. By travelling to Tokyo and talking to locals.

4. What brought Panto to Japan in 2015?

   a. A Japanese Language Aptitude Test scholarship.
   b. A Ministry of Education scholarship.
   c. A University of Tsukuba scholarship.
   d. A medical practitioners scholarship.

5. What worries Dr. Panto about Japan?

   a. He feels psychiatrists are poorly trained.
   b. He is concerned that no one has researched *hikikomori*.
   c. He is alarmed by high suicide rates.
   d. He thinks young people watch too many anime.

本文の内容に合致するものにT（True）、合致しないものにF（False）をつけなさい。

(   )   **1.** Panto was attracted to Japanese anime.

(   )   **2.** Panto started learning Japanese by listening to a CD.

(   )   **3.** Panto received a Ministry of Education Scholarship to study Japanese anime.

(   )   **4.** Panto is concerned about falling suicide rates in Japan.

(   )   **5.** Panto is worried that mental health troubles seem to be ignored in Japan.

Vocabulary

次の1～8は、「mind」に関する英文です。日本文に合うように、下の語群の中から最も適切な語を1つ選び、（   ）内に記入しなさい。

1. 大きなお世話だよ。
Mind your own (   )!

2. 何を心配しているの？
I wonder what is (   ) your mind?

3. 段差に気を付けて。
Mind the (   )!

4. もっとビール飲んで良い？
Do you mind (   ) I have some more beer?

5. 野球の選手になる夢で一杯だ。
His mind is filled (   ) dreams of becoming a baseball player.

6. 気にしないで、10分もすればもう1台来るよ。
(   ) mind, there will be another one in ten minutes.

7. 完全に忘れていた。
It completely (   ) my mind.

8. 世界一周旅行をしようと決心した。
I made (   ) my mind to travel around the world.

business	gap	if	never	on	slipped	up	with

●関東大震災時の「災害映像」発見

（東京大震火災の実況）両国国技館に避難者の群衆　　　提供：MeijiShowa／アフロ

Before you read

Questions

1. What do you think the article will be about?

   この記事は何の話題についてだと思いますか？

2. What do you know about the Great Kanto Earthquake of 1923?

   関東大震災について何か知っていますか？

次の１～５の語の説明として最も近いものをa～eから１つ選び、（　）内に記入しなさい。

1.	catastrophe	（　　）	**a.**	size or extent
2.	mayhem	（　　）	**b.**	gift to help someone
3.	magnitude	（　　）	**c.**	filmed material
4.	footage	（　　）	**d.**	disaster
5.	donation	（　　）	**e.**	disorder

Summary

次の英文は記事の要約です。下の語群から最も適切な語を１つ選び、（　）内に記入しなさい。

1-62

The 100th anniversary of the Great Kanto Earthquake will be (　　　　　) by a new (　　　　　　). It focuses on three cameramen who captured raw (　　　　　) of the 1923 catastrophe. They filmed desperate reactions to the (　　　　　) in order to encourage others to help. The film includes audio (　　　　　) from one of the cameramen.

chaos　　commentary　　documentary　　footage　　marked

　関東大震災は、1923年（大正12年）９月１日11時58分32秒に発生し、今年100年となる。本地震のマグニチュードは7.9と推定されたが、日本国外の地震波形を解析するとM8以上となる傾向がある。この地震により神奈川県および東京都を中心に、茨城県・千葉県から静岡県東部までの内陸と沿岸に及ぶ広い範囲に甚大な被害をもたらした。

　190万人が被災、死者・行方不明者は推定10万5,000人で、明治以降の日本の地震被害としては最大規模の被害となった。焼死が多かったのは、強風が関東地方に吹き込み、木造住宅が密集していた東京で火災が広範囲に発生したからである。また、正午前の食事の準備のために火を使っている家庭も多かった。水道管の破裂もあり、火災が３日間続いた。津波の発生による被害は、太平洋沿岸の相模湾沿岸部と房総半島沿岸部で発生し、高さ10m以上の津波が記録された。この震災の記録映像として、記録映画の写真家の白井茂氏による『関東大震大火実況』が残されている。また横浜シネマ商会による『横浜大震火災惨状』も所蔵されている。

Reading

1-63

A documentary on the Great Kanto Earthquake of 1923 has unearthed Japan's first 'disaster footage'

KYODO — With this year marking the 100th anniversary of the Great Kanto Earthquake, a documentary film is being produced focusing on three cameramen who captured raw and confronting footage from Tokyo in the immediate aftermath
5 of the 1923 catastrophe.

Filmed at a time when even still photography was relatively rare, the moving images taken by the three are an invaluable historical record as they provide insight into disaster response at the time while showing the widespread
10 fires and the residents' reactions amid the mayhem.

1-64

The documentary, titled "Men with Cameras: Filming the Great Kanto Earthquake," expected for release this summer, is a production by the Documentary Film Preservation Center in Tokyo.

15 "It is miraculous that footage of this time exists," says Hideyo Murayama, director general of the center. "The three young men captured images of the disaster, without regard to the dangers involved, and their selfless efforts are evident."

The three cameramen were Toshimitsu Kosaka, a then-
20 19-year-old cinematographer at Nikkatsu Mukojima Studios; Shigeru Shirai, 24, of Tokyo Cinema Shokai; and Tatsumi Iwaoka, 30, who ran a film company called Iwaoka Shokai.

1-65

The 7.9-magnitude Great Kanto quake occurred shortly before noon on Sept. 1, 1923.

25 Many buildings collapsed across the Kanto region centering Tokyo, while fires, tsunami and landslides occurred in various areas.

The number of dead and missing totaled approximately 105,000, with the casualties mainly clustered in the Kanto
30 region. Fires alone accounted for about 92,000 deaths.

Great Kanto Earthquake：
関東大震災

'disaster footage'：「災害映像」

KYODO：共同通信《世界中のメディアにニュースを配信する通信社名》

confronting：恐ろしい

catastrophe：大災害

still photography：静止画

moving images：動画

insight into ～：～の様子

mayhem：騒乱

Documentary Film Preservation Center：記録フィルム保存センター

director general of the center：センター長

without regard to ～：～を顧みずに

selfless：無私の

cinematographer：撮影監督

Nikkatsu Mukojima Studios：日活向島撮影所

Tokyo Cinema Shokai：東京シネマ商会

Iwaoka Shokai：岩岡商会

collapsed：倒壊した

landslides：土砂崩れ

casualties：死傷者

clustered in ～：～に集中した

Kosaka, who at the time of the earthquake was shooting a dramatic film, went to the Asakusa area, Tokyo's former entertainment district, to capture footage. Carrying the film reels, he traveled to Kyoto for a screening.

35 Shirai, who was in what is now Kumagaya, Saitama Prefecture, took a day to return to Tokyo and film in Nihonbashi and other areas.

1-66

The documentary traces the path Iwaoka traveled, about which little is known. After analyzing individual film 40 frames, looking at the angle of the sunlight hitting the faces of passersby and comparing the remaining buildings, it was determined that Iwaoka filmed in Asakusa and Ueno, among other locations.

The film is expected to run about 80 minutes and will 45 include audio commentary from Shirai reflecting on the time of the disaster.

After being criticized for filming the tragedy as it unfolded, Shirai defended the decision, explaining that it was not done lightly.

50 "We were shooting to encourage people to send food from rural areas (to Tokyo)," he says about the footage.

1-67

According to Murayama, more than 20 film reels about the 1923 disaster were found and they were shown in various locations in Japan, with the most dramatic portions edited 55 together, regardless of whose camera filmed them.

"The images showed the expressions on people's faces and even the movement of the flames, and it must have had a considerable impact on the people in the rural areas," says Kazushige Mashiyama, curator at the Board of Education in 60 Chuo Ward and an expert on the Great Kanto quake. "This was also necessary to collect donations from them."

The Japan Times (Kyodo), April 21, 2023

shooting 〜：〜を撮影して いた

entertainment district：歓 楽街

determined that 〜：〜と いうことが判明した

reflecting 〜：〜を振り返る

tragedy as it unfolded：悲 劇が展開する様子

it was not done lightly： 撮影が軽々しく行われた ものではない

encourage 〜 to …：〜に …するよう促す
rural areas：農村部

curator：学芸員

Board of Education：教育 委員会

Chuo Ward：中央区

donations：寄付

Exercises

Multiple Choice

次の１〜３の英文を完成させ、４〜５の英文の質問に答えるために、ａ〜ｄの中から最も適切なものを１つ選びなさい。

1. We are told that around 92,000 people

   a. lost their lives from fire.
   b. were killed in total.
   c. died from fires, tsunami and landslides.
   d. survived the disaster.

2. The writer says Kosaka showed his footage of the earthquake

   a. in Asakusa.
   b. in Nihonbashi.
   c. in Kyoto.
   d. in Saitama Prefecture.

3. The documentary includes audio from

   a. the youngest of the three cameramen.
   b. all three cameramen.
   c. Tatsumi Iwaoka and Hideyo Murayama.
   d. Shigeru Shirai.

4. What is the focus of this documentary film?

   a. The history of Tokyo before the earthquake.
   b. The reconstruction of Tokyo after the earthquake.
   c. The lives of the survivors of the earthquake.
   d. Three cameramen who filmed after the earthquake.

5. How did Shirai justify filming the terrible tragedy?

   a. It could help prevent future earthquakes.
   b. It was an opportunity to try out the latest cinematic techniques.
   c. It aimed at encouraging food donations.
   d. It captured the expressions on victims' faces.

本文の内容に合致するものにT（True）、合致しないものにF（False）をつけなさい。

(   )   **1.**   Shirai shot a disaster film in Saitama Prefecture.

(   )   **2.**   The photographers captured images of the Great Kanto Earthquake.

(   )   **3.**   Under 92 thousand people lost their lives from the Great Kanto Earthquake.

(   )   **4.**   At the time, those filming the earthquake were widely admired.

(   )   **5.**   Fewer than 20 reels of film of the disaster survive.

Vocabulary

次の1～8は、「防災」に関する英文です。日本文に合うように、適切な語を下の語群から1つ選び、（　）内に記入しなさい。

1. 備えあれば憂いなし。
(　　　　　　　) is preventing.

2. 後悔先に立たず。
What is done cannot be (　　　　　).

3. 覆水盆に返らず。
It is no use crying over (　　　　　) milk.

4. 前もって災害に備えておくのは大事なことです。
It is important to (　　　　　　) for a natural disaster beforehand.

5. 防災グッズの用意をしましたか？
Did you prepare the disaster (　　　　　) goods?

6. 南海トラフ地震に備えて防災訓練が行われます。
A disaster (　　　　　　) is going to be held in preparation for a Nankai Trough Earthquake.

7. 知事は東京の防災対策を強化すると約束した。
The governor has promised she will reinforce (　　　　　) prevention measures in Tokyo.

8. 本日防災訓練があります。
There is an (　　　　　) drill today.

disaster	drill	emergency	prepare
prevention	providing	spilt	undone

Unit 12

- ●決勝戦が日米対決となり、世界中が既に大盛り上がり
- ●日本　WBC 優勝に沸く

2023WBC 準決勝、日本対メキシコ戦で、9 回裏日本無死一塁、サヨナラ適時二塁打を放った村上宗隆選手（中央）はチームメートの祝福を受けながら歓喜のポーズ　写真：MEXSPORT ／アフロ

Before you read

Ball Park

　a～oは、野球場に関する語句です。それぞれ該当するものをイラスト①～⑮の中から選び、（　　）内に記入しなさい。

a.	mound	（　）
b.	home plate	（　）
c.	batter's box	（　）
d.	catcher's box	（　）
e.	first base	（　）
f.	second base	（　）
g.	shortstop	（　）
h.	third base	（　）
i.	left field	（　）
j.	center field	（　）
k.	right field	（　）
l.	foul line	（　）
m.	centerfield screen	（　）
n.	dugout	（　）
o.	scoreboard	（　）

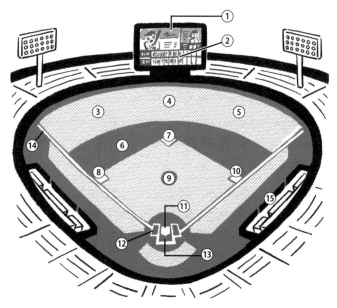

次の１〜５の語の説明として最も近いものをa〜eから１つ選び、（　　）内に記入しなさい。

1. championship （　　）　　**a** crazy enthusiasm
2. defend （　　）　　**b.** fight to retain a title
3. thriller （　　）　　**c.** series of games
4. victory （　　）　　**d.** exciting game
5. frenzy （　　）　　**e.** win

Summary

次の英文は記事の要約です。下の語群から最も適切な語を１つ選び、（　　）内に記入しなさい。

1-68
　　In a（　　　　　　）WBC semifinal against Mexico, Murakami hit a game-winning double. Japan then defeated the U.S. in the final, with Ohtani （　　　　） MVP of the tournament. While TV-viewing figures （　　　　）, many fans thronged stadiums to watch live games without COVID-19 （　　　　）. Fans' frenzied purchasing of team gear （　　　　　） to an economic boost estimated at around ¥60 billion.

added　　close　　named　　restrictions　　soared

　　野球の国・地域別対抗戦 WBC（World Baseball Classic）は2023年３月21日にアメリカ・フロリダ州マイアミの Loan Depot Park で決勝が行われ、日本代表「侍ジャパン」がアメリカを３対２で破り、2006年の第１回大会と2009年の第２回大会以来、３大会ぶりに３度目の優勝を飾った。日本は１次ラウンドから７戦全勝で世界一を奪還した。大会の最優秀選手 MVP には、投打の「二刀流」で活躍した Angels の大谷翔平選手が選ばれた。３年も続いたコロナ禍、さらにロシアのウクライナ侵攻と経済的にも社会的にも心身ともに落ち込んでいるときに、WBC の優勝は、日本中を歓喜の渦に包んだ。普段はライバル同士の選手たちが、日の丸を背負って共に優勝を目指す姿は、皆の胸を打った。
　　この第５回大会は2021年に開催予定だったが、新型コロナウイルス感染症の影響で、2023年に延期された。本選出場枠が20チームに拡大され、第１ラウンドは各組５チームによるリーグ戦方式が採用され、各組上位２チーム・計８チームによる決勝トーナメントが行われた。観客動員数は130万人を超え、決勝戦後もお祭り騒ぎとなり、日米ファン、敗退したチームのファンも輪に加わっていた。また日本国内の視聴率が40％を超え、過去最高を更新した。SNS を通じた情報発信がファンの関心をさらに高めたようだ。

Reading

1-69

With Japan-U.S. Final at the W.B.C., the World Has Already Won

MIAMI — The games in this World Baseball Classic, collectively, have been like the very best postseason series, with the mayhem unspooling so fast that you cannot possibly keep it all together.

5 Now we come to the end, on Tuesday night, when the United States will try to defend its 2017 title against Japan, which won the first two tournaments in 2006 and 2009. Japan never led in Monday's semifinal against Mexico until the moment the game ended, on a two-run double by Munetaka
10 Murakami that capped a 6-5 thriller.

1-70

The first batter was Randy Arozarena, a born showman who defected from Cuba in 2015 and has reveled in wearing the colors of Mexico, the country that gave him a home and made him a citizen. He later scaled the wall for a homer,
15 lashed a clutch double and posed like a statue after both. Here, though, he whiffed on a 101.8-mile-an-hour fastball from Roki Sasaki.

1-71

He's 21 years old and threw a perfect game with 19 strikeouts last season. You'll be hearing a lot more about him
20 in a few years — but for now, of course, the biggest Japanese star is Shohei Ohtani of the Los Angeles Angels. Ohtani led off the bottom of the ninth by drilling the first pitch for a double, and scored on Murakami's winning hit.

On Tuesday, though, those U.S. mashers will face the
25 starter Shota Imanaga, and then likely Yu Darvish, the ace of the San Diego Padres, who can beat any lineup. And among the other available relievers just might be that Ohtani fellow.

Tyler Kepner
The New York Times, March 21, 2023

MIAMI：マイアミ《フロリダ州》

World Baseball Classic：《野球の世界一を決める国別大会》

mayhem：大騒ぎ、興奮

keep ～ all together：～をひとまとめにする

two-run double：2点タイムリー2塁打

Munetaka Murakami：村上宗隆

capped ～：～の最後を締めくくる→サヨナラ勝ち

thriller：ワクワクするゲーム→接戦

defected from ～：～から亡命した

reveled in ～：～を楽しんだ

scaled the wall for a homer：フェンスをよじ登ってホームラン性の当たりを捕った

lashed a clutch double：激走して2塁打を摑んだ

posed like a statue：仁王立ちした

whiffed on ～：～を空振り三振した

Roki Sasaki：佐々木朗希

Shohei Ohtani：大谷翔平

led off ～：～の先頭打者だった

Shota Imanaga：今永昇太

Yu Darvish：ダルビッシュ有

Japan's World Baseball Classic glory spurs fan frenzy at home

30   As Japan stormed through the competition on the way to victory in the World Baseball Classic, record numbers of fans packed stadiums in Tokyo, with others waiting in long lines to buy Samurai Japan gear.

     Official fan gear for Japan's star players remains out of
35 stock, with potential buyers reportedly having to wait months to get their hands on shirts emblazoned with the numbers of players like pitcher Yu Darvish and two-way phenom Shohei Ohtani.

     Fans thronged stadiums to watch Japan's games in person,
40 too, free of the COVID-19 restrictions that limited attendance at sporting events in recent years. Combined, some 361,976 fans attended the 10 games in the Pool B round, which included Japan, at Tokyo Dome, the most attended round in the competition's history, according to the WBC.

45   For the final game between Japan and the U.S. on Wednesday morning, the average broadcast viewership in the Kanto region was around 42.4%, peaking at 46% when Ohtani struck out his Los Angeles Angels teammate Mike Trout in a dream matchup, according to a preliminary survey by Video
50 Research.

     Ohtani, who was picked as the MVP for the tournament, reportedly gained more than 2 million followers on Instagram during the two-week event, becoming the first Major League Baseball player to top 4 million followers.

55   The enthusiasm, excitement and drama was just what the nation needed, with the economic impact from Japan winning the WBC championship estimated to be about ¥59.6 billion, according to Katsuhiro Miyamoto, a professor emeritus at Kansai University.

Kathleen Benoza
The Japan Times, March 23, 2023

---

stormed through ～ on the way to … : ～で…への道を切り開いた

gear : グッズ

numbers : 背番号

phenom : 天才

in person : 直接

free of ～ : ～から解放されて

preliminary survey : 速報

Video Research :《企業名》

MVP : 最優秀選手

Instagram :《SNS の企業名》

top ～ : ～を超える

enthusiasm : 熱狂

impact from ～ : ～による興奮

estimated to ～ : ～と推定された

Katsuhiro Miyamoto : 宮本勝弘

Exercises

Multiple Choice

次の１〜５の英文の質問に答えるために、ａ〜ｄの中から最も適切なものを１つ選びなさい。

1. Who won the first two World Baseball Classic tournaments?

    a. Mexico
    b. The United States
    c. Japan
    d. Cuba

2. Who hit the winning two-run double in Japan's semifinal game?

    a. Shohei Ohtani
    b. Yu Darvish
    c. Randy Arozarena
    d. Munetaka Murakami

3. What is Randy Arozarena's native country?

    a. Cuba
    b. The United States
    c. Mexico
    d. Brazil

4. What was the average crowd size at each of the 10 games at Tokyo Dome?

    a. Around 360,000.
    b. Around 36,000.
    c. About 42.4%.
    d. About 46%.

5. What did Professor Miyamoto say about the tournament's economic impact?

    a. It cost Japan nearly ¥60 billion.
    b. It was timely and beneficial.
    c. It was not as much as he had hoped.
    d. It was negative because the stores ran out of goods.

本文の内容に合致するものにＴ（True）、合致しないものにＦ（False）をつけなさい。

(　) **1.** The American team wanted to defend its 2017 title.

(　) **2.** Munetaka Murakami hit the winning two-run double in Japan's final game against Mexico.

(　) **3.** Randy Arozarena as the first batter missed a swing on Roki Sasaki's fastball in the semifinal game.

(　) **4.** More than 365,000 fans attended the ten games including Japan at Tokyo Dome.

(　) **5.** Shohei Ohtani struck out Mike Trout in the final game.

Vocabulary

次の１〜８は、野球に関する英文です。下のＡ〜Ｈの語群の中から［　］内、そしてａ〜ｈの和訳語の中からそれぞれ最も適切なものを１つ選び、（　）内に記入しなさい。

1. [　] is a substitute athlete who seldom plays. (　)
2. [　] can both score and defend. (　)
3. [　] is a home run and gets four points. (　)
4. [　] is the area in a baseball field used by pitchers to get ready to play. (　)
5. [　] is a left-handed pitcher. (　)
6. [　] is played between the Central League and the Pacific League. (　)
7. [　] is going first before the others. (　)
8. [　] is a hit which allows the batter to reach second base. (　)

A. A bench warmer　**B.** A bullpen　**C.** A double　**D.** A grand slam
E. An interplay game　**F.** A leadoff　**G.** A southpaw　**H.** A two-way player

a. 先頭打者　　　**b.** 左腕投手　　**c.** 二塁打　　**d.** 交流試合
e. 満塁ホームラン　**f.** 控え選手　　**g.** ブルペン　**h.** 二刀流選手

Unit **13**

●中国を拒否し続ける台湾同盟国

台湾支持を辞めて中国に寝返る国が増える中、様々な理由で、中国を拒否
し続け、台湾との同盟を堅持し続ける国もある　　　　提供：アフロ

Before you read

Taiwan　台湾
面積　36,000km²（九州より少し小さい）
人口　23,400,000人／**主要都市**　台北、台中、高雄
言語　中国語、台湾語、客家語／**識字率**　98.3%
民族　台湾原住の本省人　85%／中国本土からの外省人　15%
宗教　道教　4％／仏教　0.6%
　　　キリスト教　1.1%
　　　（カトリック　0.9%／プロテスタント　0.2%）
通貨　新台湾ドル／**政体**　民主共和制
GDP　7,727億米ドル／1人当たりの GDP　33,004米ドル

Belize　ベリーズ
面積　22,966km²／**人口**　398,000人／**首都**　ベルモパン
公用語　英語／**識字率**　82.7%
民族　メスティーソ　48.7%／ベリーズ・クレオール　24.9%
宗教　キリスト教　72%
　　　（カトリック　40%／プロテスタント　32%）
GDP　28億米ドル／1人当たりの GDP　8,013米ドル

Guatemala　グアテマラ
面積　108,889km²（北海道と四国を合わせた広さ）
人口　17,910,000人／**主要都市**　グアテマラ
言語　スペイン語／**識字率**　70%
民族　マヤ系　42%／メスティーソ　56%
宗教　キリスト教（カトリック　67%／プロテスタント　33%）
通貨　ケツアル／**政体**　立憲共和制
GDP　767億米ドル／1人当たりの GDP　8,303米ドル

次の1〜5の語の説明として最も近いものをa〜eから1つ選び、（　　）内に記入しなさい。

1.	ally	（　　）	**a.**	obligation
2.	renegotiate	（　　）	**b.**	try to change an agreement
3.	debt	（　　）	**c.**	respond aggressively
4.	retaliate	（　　）	**d.**	partner
5.	statehood	（　　）	**e.**	status as independent country

Summary

　次の英文は記事の要約です。下の語群から最も適切な語を1つ選び、（　　）内に記入しなさい。

1-74

　　When Honduras cut diplomatic (　　　　　　) with Taiwan, it left the island with just 13 formal diplomatic (　　　　　　). Since 2016, nine countries have (　　　　　　) allegiance to China under economic and political pressure from Beijing. Taiwanese financial support is a major (　　　　　　) for the remaining 13 countries. But some of them also have (　　　　　　) reasons for staying loyal.

allies	ideological	motivation	switched	ties

　　南米で唯一台湾と外交関係をもつパラグアイの大統領選挙は与党候補が勝利し、今後も台湾との関係が維持される見通しとなった。任期満了に伴うパラグアイの大統領選挙は2023年4月30日投票が行われた。今回の選挙では、台湾との外交関係を維持するかどうかが争点の1つになり、右派の与党候補で元財務相のサンティアゴ・ペニャが台湾との関係維持を主張した。中道の野党連合の候補で元下院議長のエフライン・アレグレは、農産物の輸出拡大のため台湾と外交関係を断絶して、新たに中国と国交を結ぶ可能性を示唆してきた。

　　パラグアイは、台湾が外交関係をもつ13か国のうちの1つで、南米大陸では唯一の国だ。ペニャは44歳で、学生時代、台湾の奨学金で現地の起業家向けの研修に参加した経験がある。パラグアイは人口に占める若者の割合が大きく、若者の支持が選挙の勝敗を大きく左右した。「若者の教育や雇用の創出に力を入れてほしい」といった若者を重視した政策に期待する声も聞かれた。また、中南米では、2023年3月、ホンジュラスが台湾と外交関係を断絶するなど、中国と国交を結ぶ国が相次いでいた。

Reading

'Not about the highest bidder': the countries defying China to stick with Taiwan

Outside an unmarked building on the banks of a Taipei river, 14 flags usually fly, one for each of Taiwan's allies. But last week, the flag of Honduras was removed from the site, which houses diplomatic outposts. Now, just 13 remain.

5 The standard came down after Xiomara Castro, the president of Honduras, announced on Twitter she was making good on promises made during her campaign to cut diplomatic ties with Taiwan after 82 years and ally with China.

The country's foreign minister said Honduras was
10 struggling financially and Taiwan hadn't answered a request to renegotiate $600m in debt or increase financial aid. Taiwan accused Honduras of asking for more than $2bn and urged it not to "quench your thirst with poison" by siding with China.

Nine countries have switched allegiance to China since
15 Tsai Ing-wen became president in 2016 and Beijing increased its efforts to diplomatically isolate Taiwan. It leaves just 13 formal diplomatic allies. The weight on their shoulders is heavy, as is the price they can pay for not siding with China, which doesn't allow its allies to also recognise Taiwan.

20 Taiwan's remaining allies are Belize, Guatemala, Haiti, Paraguay, Saint Kitts and Nevis, Saint Lucia, and Saint Vincent and the Grenadines in the Americas. In the Pacific, it is still recognised by the Marshall Islands, Nauru, Palau and Tuvalu. Eswatini is its only African ally, and Vatican City the
25 only one in Europe.

The countries each have their individual histories, reasons and motivations for deciding to ally with Taiwan.

"We've hitched our sovereignty to Taiwan. We're saying we're standing by you," says the St Vincent and the Grenadines
30 ambassador, Andrea Clare Bowman.

The Caribbean nation, home to about 104,000 people,

---

bidder：入札者

defying ～ to …：～が…するのを拒否する

stick with ～：～に固執する

Taipei：台北の《台湾の首都》

allies：同盟国

diplomatic outposts：外交前哨基地

standard：（儀式用の）旗

making good on promises：約束を果たしている

campaign：選挙活動

cut diplomatic ties with ～：～との外交関係を断つ

accused ～ of …：～が…したと非難した

quench your thirst with ～：喉の渇きを～で癒す

siding with ～：～に味方して

allegiance to ～：～への忠誠・支持

Tsai Ing-wen：蔡英文

president：総統

isolate ～：～を孤立させる

as is the price：代償も大きい

Americas：南北両アメリカ大陸

Vatican City：バチカン市国

hitched ～ to …：～を…に連結させる

sovereignty：主権

---

opened its embassy in Taipei in 2019, the same year it became the smallest country ever to sit on the United Nations security council, alongside China. Last August, its prime minister,
35 Ralph Gonsalves, visited Taiwan in the midst of China's live-fire military drills, retaliating against US House Speaker Nancy Pelosi's visit.

Tuvalu's decision in 1979 to side with Taiwan was made largely out of ideology and faith: the deeply Christian country
40 was wary of the communists, says Tuvalu's ambassador, Bikenibau Paeniu.

St Lucia has formed ties with Taiwan twice, most recently returning to Taiwan in 2007 after it increased its aid and assistance.

45 Its ambassador, Dr. Robert Kennedy Lewis, says his government would say "its foreign policy is not about the highest bidder" but adds that Taiwan is now its biggest donor of grant aid.

At the end of this current semester, 170 Honduran students
50 in Taiwan will lose their scholarships, and likely have to return home with unfinished degrees.

The transactional nature of its alliances is debated within Taiwan, but allies say they give international legitimacy to its statehood, and give Taipei a voice on the world stage.

55 That voice could become fainter as soon as next month, when Taiwan faces the loss of another friendly country. Paraguay's opposition party has said it will switch to Beijing if it wins the presidential election on 30 April, citing trade opportunities.

Helen Davidson
The Guardian, April 4, 2023

United Nations security council：国連安全保障理事会

live-fire military drills：実弾軍事演習

retaliating against 〜：〜に仕返しする

US House Speaker：米下院議長

visit：（台湾）訪問

wary of 〜：〜を警戒する

donor of grant aid：無償援助供与国

with unfinished degrees：学位を取得せずに

give legitimacy to its statehood：（相手国に）国家としての正当性を与える

opposition party：野党

Exercises

次の１〜５の英文の質問に答えるために、ａ〜ｄの中から最も適切なものを１つ選びなさい。

1. What does the sign say on the building where the flags are flown?

    a. It currently says "Embassy of Honduras."

    b. It used to say "Embassy of Honduras."

    c. It says "Diplomatic Outpost."

    d. It does not appear to have a sign.

2. What seems to be the main reason Honduras changed its policy?

    a. It owes $600m to China.

    b. It owes more than $2bn to Taiwan.

    c. The country was dissatisfied with the financial support it got from Taiwan.

    d. The new president's family had supported China for 82 years.

3. How many countries had diplomatic relations with Taiwan in 2016?

    a. 13.

    b. 14.

    c. 22.

    d. 24.

4. Where are most of the countries that still support Taiwan?

    a. They are mostly in Asia.

    b. They are spread evenly around the world.

    c. They are in Central America and the Pacific.

    d. They are in Africa or Europe.

5. According to Ms. Bowman, why does her country have diplomatic ties with Taiwan?

    a. To be able to argue effectively with China on the UN Security Council.

    b. To benefit from the increased aid that Taiwan offered.

    c. To support Christianity and oppose communism.

    d. To show its solidarity with the island.

本文の内容に合致するものにT（True）、合致しないものにF（False）をつけなさい。

(   ) **1.** Xiomara Castro tried to continue diplomatic ties with Taiwan.

(   ) **2.** Saint Lucia and Saint Vincent are allies with China.

(   ) **3.** Bikenibau Paeniu was cautious of the communists.

(   ) **4.** Honduran students who study in Taiwan will no longer have scholarships.

(   ) **5.** Ralph Consalves visited Taiwan while China did military drills.

Vocabulary

次の１～６は、カリブ海諸国に関する英文です。下記の国名から１つ選び（   ）内に、a～fを地図から選び、[   ]内に記入しなさい。

1. (   ) is a microstate consisting of the two islands.   [   ]

2. (   ) is an island country and its capital is Kingstown.   [   ]

3. (   )'s capital is Roseau and its main language is English. [   ]

4. (   ) is called Isle of Spice and its capital is St. George's.   [   ]

5. (   ) is located about 39km south of Martinique.   [   ]

6. (   )'s people are called Barbadian.   [   ]

Barbados	Dominica	Grenada
Saint Kitts and Nevis	Saint Lucia	Saint Vincent

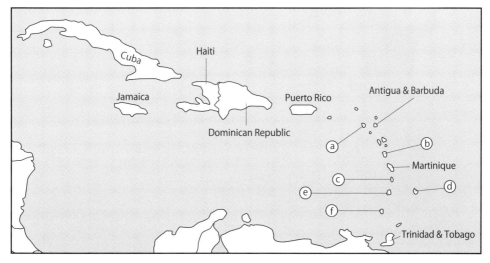

Unit 14

●フィンランドの NATO 加盟発表とロシア国境

フィンランドが NATO 加盟を発表すると、ロシアがすぐさま軍隊の増派を発表するなど、両国の国境地帯に緊張が走る中、フィンランドのイマトゥラ州ペルコラ近くを警戒するフィンランド国境警備隊員　　　　　　　　写真：AFP ／アフロ

Before you read

Republic of Finland
フィンランド共和国

面積　338,000km²（日本よりやや小さい）（世界64位）
人口　5,541,000人（世界116位）
首都　ヘルシンキ
言語　フィンランド語
　　　（全人口の5.2%スウェーデン語）
識字率　99%
民族　フィン人　91.7%
　　　スウェーデン人　5.5%
宗教　キリスト教・福音ルーテル派　78%
　　　キリスト教・フィンランド正教会　1.1%
　　　無宗教　20%
GDP　2,742億ドル（世界44位）
　　　１人当たり GDP　49,738ドル（世界15位）
通貨　ユーロ
政体　共和制

次の1～5の語句の説明として最も近いものをa～eから1つ選び、（　）内に記入しなさい。

1. bolster　　　　（　　）　　　**a.** move, reposition

2. deploy　　　　（　　）　　　**b.** complete or official

3. ratify　　　　（　　）　　　**c.** approve, confirm

4. emphasise　　（　　）　　　**d.** strengthen

5. full-fledged　（　　）　　　**e.** highlight

次の英文は記事の要約です。下の語群から最も適切な語を1つ選び、（　）内に記入しなさい。

2-01

　　Finland's NATO (　　　　　　　) marks the end of a process that began in May 2022, following Russia's (　　　　　　) of Ukraine. While Turkey has ratified Finland's (　　　　　　), it continues to delay Sweden's bid, as does Hungary. While NATO officials work hard to bring Sweden into the (　　　　　), Russia says it will strengthen its (　　　　　) defenses.

accession	alliance	application	border	invasion

　　フィンランドが2023年4月4日、北大西洋条約機構NATOの31番目の加盟国になった。中立を外交防衛方針としていたフィンランドは、ロシアのウクライナ侵攻をきっかけにNATO加盟へと動いた。フィンランドのサウリ・ニーニスト大統領は、「同盟に加盟することで、フィンランドは安全保障を得られる。他方でフィンランドは同盟に安全保障を提供する。フィンランドは、NATOの全加盟国の安全保障に強くかかわり、地域安定を強化する信頼できる同盟国となる」と述べた。

　　フィンランドは、1300km以上に渡り、ロシアと国境を接している。第2次世界大戦でソ連との戦争に敗れた経験から、ソ連、ロシアとの安定的な関係を優先し、軍事的な中立政策をとってきた。しかし、NATO加盟という歴史的な政策転換に踏み出した。「フィンランドは行動が安定して予見しやすい北欧の国で、紛争の平和的解決を目指す。フィンランドにとって重要な原則や価値は、今後も我々の外交の指針となる」と大統領は強調した。さらに、「NATOの集団的抑止と防衛にフィンランドが最も大きく貢献するには、自国の領土の安全保障と防衛が基礎となるのは明らかだ」と述べた。

Reading

2-02

Finland to join Nato on Tuesday as Russia sounds border warning

Russia has said it will bolster its defences near its 1,300km border with Finland after the Nato secretary general, Jens Stoltenberg, announced that the Nordic country would formally join the transatlantic defence alliance on Tuesday.

5　　The accession marks the end of an accelerated process that began last May, when Finland and neighbouring Sweden abandoned decades of military nonalignment to seek security as Nato members after Russia's invasion of Ukraine.

2-03

　　Turkey last week became the last of the alliance's 30
10　member states to ratify Finland's application, but Turkey and Hungary continue to hold up Sweden's bid. Stockholm said last week it was not sure it would join in time for a planned Nato summit in July.

　　"Tomorrow we will welcome Finland as the 31st member
15　of Nato, making Finland safer and our alliance stronger," Stoltenberg said in Brussels on Monday. "We will raise the Finnish flag for the first time here at Nato headquarters."

　　Finland's accession was "good for Finland's security, for Nordic security and for Nato as a whole," he added. "President
20　Putin went to war against Ukraine with the clear aim to get less Nato. He's getting the exact opposite."

2-04

　　The Finnish president, Sauli Niinistö, and the foreign minister, Pekka Haavisto, will travel to Brussels to take part in the ceremony. "It is a historic moment for us," Haavisto
25　said in a statement after Stoltenberg's announcement.

　　"For Finland, the most important objective at the meeting will be to emphasise Nato's support to Ukraine as Russia continues its illegal aggression. We seek to promote stability and security throughout the Euro-Atlantic region."

30　　In Moscow, Russia's deputy foreign minister, Alexander Grushko, responded to the news of Finland's accession

---

to join:《見出し中、動詞が to 不定詞の場合、未来を表す。同様に過去分詞の場合は受動態を表す》

Nato：北大西洋条約機構《本部はベルギーのブリュッセル》

sounds 〜：〜を発する

secretary general：事務総長

Nordic：北欧の

accession：加盟

military nonalignment：軍事非同盟

ratify 〜：〜を批准する

application：申請

bid：試み

in time for 〜：〜に間に合って

went to war against 〜：〜に対して戦争を行った

with the clear aim：明確な目的をもって

get less 〜：〜の数を減らす

statement：声明

aggression：侵略

seek to 〜：〜を目指す

Euro-Atlantic region：ユーロ大西洋地域

deputy：副

---

by saying Russia would increase its forces in its west and northwestern regions if necessary.

If the "forces and resources of other Nato members are deployed in Finland, we will take additional steps to reliably ensure Russia's military security" by "strengthening our military potential in the west and in the northwest," Grushko said.

Turkey continues to delay Sweden's accession, arguing that Stockholm is sheltering members of what Ankara considers terrorist groups — a charge Sweden denies — and has demanded their extradition as a step toward ratifying Swedish membership.

Relations were also hit by a demonstration in January near the Turkish embassy in Stockholm at which a far-right politician burned a copy of the Qur'an. Sweden has said it takes Turkey's allegations seriously.

Sweden's foreign minister, Tobias Billström, said last week he was no longer confident that his country would be able to join the alliance by July, after fresh objections from Hungary. "I think 'hopeful' in this context is better," Billstrom said.

Hungary also objects to unspecified "grievances" over past Swedish criticisms of prime minister Viktor Orbán's policies. Stoltenberg said Nato was working hard to get Sweden on board as soon as possible.

Officials are keen to bring Sweden in before US president Joe Biden and other alliance leaders meet in the Lithuanian capital, Vilnius, on 11 and 12 July. "Sweden is not left alone. Sweden is as close as it can come as a full-fledged member," Stoltenberg said.

John Henley
The Guardian, April 3, 2023

forces：軍隊

if necessary：必要に応じて

deployed：配備される

take additional steps：追加の措置を講じる

potential：可能性、潜在力

extradition：引き渡し

Qur'an：コーラン《イスラム教の聖典》

allegations：主張

fresh：新たな

in this context：この文脈では

unspecified grievances：不特定の不満

get ～ on board：～を加入させる

keen to ～：～することを熱望する

left alone：放って置かれる、一人残される

as close as it can come：可能な限り近づいている

full-fledged：本格的な

Exercises

Multiple Choice

次の1の英文を完成させ、2〜5の英文の質問に答えるために、a〜dの中から最も適切なものを1つ選びなさい。

1. In joining the alliance, Finland's president says his country aims to

   a. strengthen defenses on its western border.

   b. show its support for Ukraine.

   c. solve its grievances with Hungary, Russia and Turkey.

   d. continue its policy of military nonalignment.

2. Which NATO countries have agreed to admit Finland but not Sweden?

   a. Most of the Nordic countries.

   b. Lithuania and the other Baltic countries.

   c. Hungary and Turkey.

   d. Russia and Ukraine.

3. What seems to be delaying Sweden's NATO entry?

   a. Stoltenberg's criticisms of the Hungarian government.

   b. Putin's desire to have "less NATO."

   c. Political tensions with some NATO member countries.

   d. Economic differences with Finland.

4. What is needed for Sweden to sit alongside other NATO members in July?

   a. The agreement of two more NATO countries.

   b. President Biden's arrival in Vilnius.

   c. The end of the war in Ukraine.

   d. Stoltenberg's appointment as NATO secretary-general.

5. According to the article, what was Russia's response to the Finnish move?

   a. Its deputy foreign minister met Stoltenberg in Brussels.

   b. It announced that it may reinforce its border militarily.

   c. Its government condemned the move as illegal aggression.

   d. It moved large numbers of troops to its border with Finland.

本文の内容に合致するものにＴ（True）、合致しないものにＦ（False）をつけなさい。

(   ) **1.** Russia and Finland share a 1,300 km-long border.

(   ) **2.** Finland became the thirty-second member state.

(   ) **3.** Finland has shown its support for Ukraine.

(   ) **4.** Hungary opposed Sweden's entry because of Swedish criticism of the Hungarian prime minister's policies.

(   ) **5.** The NATO officials are trying hard to get Turkey's agreement before July, 2023.

Vocabulary

次の１〜７は、「NATO」に関する英文です。適切な語を下の語群から１つ選び、（   ）内に記入しなさい。

1. NATO is an acronym for North (   ) Treaty (   ).

2. Currently (   ) countries are members of NATO.

3. NATO is a (   ) alliance originally established in 1949.

4. NATO was founded in response to the (   ) posed by the Soviet Union.

5. NATO serves three purposes, deterring Russian (   ), forbidding the (   ) of nationalist militarism in Europe and encouraging European political (   ).

6. Finland is the (   ) member of NATO; it joined in April, 2023.

7. Poland, Czechia and (   ) joined NATO in 1999.

Atlantic	expansionism	Hungary	integration	military
newest	Organization	revival	thirty-one	threat

●オーストラリア 「国王」戴冠式に無関心な理由

●ニュージーランド 「国王」戴冠式とマオリの人たち

「ワイタンギ協定」締結記念館でマオリの人たちから1994年以来25年ぶりに歓待を受けるチャールズ皇太子夫妻（2019年当時の写真）　写真：REX／アフロ

Before you read

New Zealand
ニュージーランド

面積　270,467km²（日本の約4の3）
人口　5,005,882人／**首都　ウエリントン**
公用語　英語（事実上）、マオリ語
識字率　99%
民族　ヨーロッパ系　74%／マオリ人　15%
　　　アジア系　11.8%／太平洋諸島系　7.4%
　　　中東系・ラテン系・アフリカ系　1.2%
宗教　キリスト教　47%／無宗教　41.9%
通貨　ニュージーランド・ドル
政体　立憲君主制
GDP　2,093億8,400万ドル
　　　1人当たりのGDP　41,164ドル

次の1〜5の語の説明として最も近いものをa〜eから1つ選び、（　）内に記入しなさい。

1. coronation （　） **a.** influence, consequence or heritage
2. monarchy （　） **b.** country ruled or represented by king, queen
3. horde （　） **c.** ceremony to appoint a monarch
4. obverse （　） **d.** face, front side
5. legacy （　） **e.** crowd

Summary

　次の英文は記事の要約です。下の語群から最も適切な語を1つ選び、（　）内に記入しなさい。

2-07

　Like his (　　　　　) mother, Queen Elizabeth, Charles III is sovereign of many countries (　　　　　) than Britain. But in both Australia and New Zealand celebrations for his (　　　　　) are muted. Although increasingly discussed, however, republicanism does not yet appear to have strong (　　　　　). Some Maoris even see the British monarchy as a guarantor of their (　　　　　) rights.

| coronation | historical | late | other | support |

　イギリスのチャールズ国王の戴冠式が2023年5月6日、ロンドンで行われた。エリザベス女王の時より簡素で多様性を重視した式典となった。2022年9月に即位したチャールズ国王は、カミラ王妃とともにロンドンのウェストミンスター寺院で戴冠式に臨んだ。チャールズ国王が、イギリスとイギリス連邦の14ヶ国を法に基づき統治することを誓ったあと、イギリス国教会の聖職者であるカンタベリー大主教の祝福などを受け、王冠が授けられた。世論調査で「君主制を支持する」と回答した人は18歳から24歳では32％と、共和制支持の38％を下回った。式典の参列者は約2200人とエリザベス女王の時の4分の1に絞られた。国王夫妻の馬車のルートも大幅に短縮された。

　イギリス連邦（Commonwealth of Nations）は、イギリス帝国のほぼ全ての旧領土である56の加盟国から構成される国家連合。20世紀前半に、イギリス帝国の脱植民地化に伴い、領土の自治が強化されたことで始まり、自由で平等なものとして56ヶ国が加盟した。首長は、チャールズ3世、君主制である加盟国20ヶ国のうち15ヶ国の元首であり、他の5つの君主国は独自の君主を持つ。他の36の加盟国は共和制である。加盟国は相互に法的義務を負っていないが、英語の使用や歴史的な繋がりがある。民主主義・人権・法の支配という共通の価値観を有している。イギリス連邦の国々の面積は21％を占め、総人口は3分の1近くに相当する。

Reading

2-08

Why the king's coronation will be a muted affair in Australia

For the coronation of King Charles III, Australians can buy a T-shirt commemorating the event.

"Democracy Not Monarchy," reads one of the offerings from the Australian Republican Movement. "One of Us. For Us. By Us." says another. "Keep the Crown" proclaims a shirt backing the status quo from the Australian Monarchist League.

As the death of his mother did, the coronation of King Charles has reanimated debate in Australia about its future governance, and the possibility the country might jettison the British royal family to become a republic.

2-09

The Australian government will be represented at the coronation ceremony in London by the prime minister, Anthony Albanese, alongside the king's representative in Australia, the governor general, David Hurley, and the governors of Australia's states.

But for those antipodean subjects of King Charles — he became King of Australia automatically at the moment of his mother's death — there appears likely to be little fanfare.

No national public holiday has been declared for the Monday, and only one state, Western Australia, has said it will "consider" giving its royal subjects the day off. Urging a national commemorative day, the Australian Monarchist League said a public holiday on 8 May would "no doubt be well received".

2-10

The League also condemned as "neo-communism in action" the Australian government's decision to exclude the new sovereign from the next $5 note. Queen Elizabeth II has featured on the note's obverse since 1992. A new note will eschew King Charles III, instead featuring a design that "honours the culture and history of the First Australians".

Ben Doherty
The Guardian, May 1, 2023

coronation：戴冠式

muted：静かな

commemorating 〜：〜を記念する

"Democracy Not Monarchy"：「君主制ではなく民主主義を」

offerings：提案

Australian Republican Movement：オーストラリア共和国運動

"One of Us. For Us. By Us."：「我々の、我々のための、我々による国」《米国独立宣言のもじり、そしてジョーン・オズボーンの曲名》

status quo：現状

Australian Monarchist League：オーストラリア君主主義者同盟

reanimated 〜：〜を復活させた

jettison 〜：〜を追放する

governor general：総督

governors：各州知事

subjects：臣民

antipodean：地球の反対側の

the Monday：国王の公式誕生日

the Australians 〜 note：《condemned の目的語》

sovereign：君主

eschew 〜：〜を避ける

First Australians：最初のオーストラリア人《アボリジニーとトレス海峡諸島民、最近のドラマのタイトル》

Tea, bunting but no magic: appeal of king's coronation shrinks in New Zealand

The crowning of a new king is expected to pass relatively quietly in New Zealand: no public holiday, no mass parades, no flag-waving hordes. As coronation planning begins to seep into talkback radio discussions and newspaper headlines, however, there are questions of whether it will prompt a wider consideration of colonial legacy in Aotearoa. "I haven't heard much discussion on the coronation … [other than] discussing the coronation quiche as an underwhelming choice for the Coronation signature dish!" says Dr Helene Connor, Head of the School of Māori and Indigenous Education at University of Auckland. "Thinking about Māori and monarchy, though, there are so many contradictions inherent in this relationship with Aotearoa, as a former colony of the British empire," she says. "Despite the effects of colonisation, many Māori remain loyal to the British monarchy and have an expectation that Queen Victoria's descendants will honour the Treaty [of Waitangi] as a Treaty partner."

King Charles occupies a complex role in New Zealand politics and history — as a primary guarantor of indigenous rights and sovereignty under the treaty of Waitangi, as well as the institution responsible for its breaches.

But New Zealand has not expressed strong appetite for republicanism: a 2022 Reid Research poll asked whether New Zealand should become a republic when Queen Elizabeth's reign ended: 48% said no, and 36.4% yes.

Tess McClure
The Guardian, April 28, 2023

Tea：ティーパーティー

bunting：祝い用の装飾

Aotearoa：アオテアオラ《ニュージーランドを指す現代マオリ語》

other than 〜：〜以外に

quiche：キッシュ《パイ料理の一種》

signature dish：特製料理

Head of the School of Māori and Indigenous Education：マオリ・先住民教育学部長

contradictions：矛盾

inherent：内在している

Treaty [of Waitangi]：ワイタンギの条約

guarantor：保証人

appetite for 〜：〜への欲求

Reid Research：《市場調査コンサルタント会社名》

Exercises

Multiple Choice

次の１〜３の英文の質問に答え、４〜５の英文を完成させるために、ａ〜ｄの中から最も適切なものを１つ選びなさい。

1. Who is offering T-shirts with the slogan "Democracy Not Monarchy"?

    a. The Australian Republican Movement.

    b. The Australian Monarchist League.

    c. The Keep the Crown Movement.

    d. The state of Western Australia.

2. How do New Zealanders feel about becoming a republic?

    a. Most are in favor of the idea.

    b. Two thirds oppose the idea.

    c. About a third support it but nearly half are against it.

    d. They worry that without a king they will become dependent on Australia.

3. How does the Australian Monarchist League regard the proposed new $5 note?

    a. They do not want Queen Elizabeth's image replaced by King Charles'.

    b. They say it represents leftwing politics.

    c. They dislike the way the king looks in the new design.

    d. They want the government to issue a coin to commemorate the coronation.

4. The two articles suggest that there is keen enthusiasm for the coronation ceremony

    a. in both Australia and New Zealand.

    b. in neither Australia nor New Zealand.

    c. in Australia, but not in New Zealand.

    d. among the First Australians.

5. According to Dr. Connor, Māori have mixed feelings about the British monarchy as

    a. they loved Queen Elizabeth but are less fond of King Charles.

    b. criticism of Charles could encourage criticism of their traditional leaders.

    c. it is associated both with colonialism and with support of their rights.

    d. they would prefer a Māori king, not a British one.

本文の内容に合致するものにＴ（True）、合致しないものにＦ（False）をつけなさい。

(   ) **1.** The Australian Republican Movement has the slogan "Keep the Crown."

(   ) **2.** King Charles became head of the Commonwealth automatically.

(   ) **3.** The new Australian $5 note will avoid depicting King Charles III.

(   ) **4.** The coronation of King Charles III has been greeted with great joy in New Zealand.

(   ) **5.** Dr. Connor felt honored to celebrate the coronation of King Charles III.

Vocabulary

次の１〜７は、「戴冠式」に関する語句です。該当する英語説明文を下のａ〜ｇの中から１つ選び、（　）に入れなさい。

1. Ascot   (   )
2. Commonwealth   (   )
3. coronation   (   )
4. crown   (   )
5. Inauguration Day   (   )
6. monarchy   (   )
7. Westminster Abbey   (   )

a. worn by a king or queen as a sign of royal power

b. government including a king or queen

c. the day an American president is accepted into office

d. an organization of about 50 independent countries which were formerly parts of the British Empire

e. almost all English kings and queens have been crowned in this Gothic church

f. a four-day horse racing event held in England every June

g. the ceremony at which a king or queen is crowned

●米国の驚異的な経済記録からの教訓

ニューヨーク証券取引所。米国経済は景気後退に入っていると思われているが、各種データを見ると、実はそうではない 写真：アフロ

Before you read

United States of America
アメリカ合衆国

面積　9,628,000km²（日本の約25.5倍）（世界3位）
人口　330,000,000人（世界3位）
首都　ワシントンDC
最大都市　ニューヨーク
公用語　なし、事実上は英語
識字率　93.5%
人種　白人　72.4%／ヒスパニック　18.5%
　　　黒人　12.7%／アジア系　4.8%
　　　ネイティブ・アメリカン　0.9%
宗教　キリスト教・カトリック　21%
　　　キリスト教・プロテスタント　58%
　　　ユダヤ教　1.3%
　　　イスラム教　0.9%
　　　無宗教　22.8%
GDP　21兆4,300億ドル（世界1位）
　　　1人当たりGDP　65,133ドル（世界11位）
通貨　USドル
政体　大統領制・連邦制

次の1～5の語の説明として最も近いものをa～eから1つ選び、（　）内に記入しなさい。

1. broken	（　）		**a.**	ungenerous
2. obscure	（　）		**b.**	in need of repair
3. enduring	（　）		**c.**	hide
4. impressive	（　）		**d.**	long-lasting
5. stingy	（　）		**e.**	remarkably good

Summary

次の英文は記事の要約です。下の語群から最も適切な語を1つ選び、（　）内に記入しなさい。

2-13

　　Despite (　　　　　　　) among liberal and conservative Americans alike, US economic growth is impressive. The world's richest and most productive big economy (　　　　　　) for 58% of the G7's GDP compared with 40% in 1990. Reasons include a young (　　　　　), immigration, and generous research (　　　　　　). While some criticize its lack of social safety nets, even its poorest state enjoys higher average (　　　　　) power than France.

accounts	investment	pessimism	purchasing	workforce

　　コロナ禍で世界の景気が後退している中で、アメリカの経済は相変わらずの強さを見せている。これほどまでに米国経済が強い理由には「人口増加・技術革新・高利益率・配当主義・個人消費」の5つがある。米国株式市場は、200年以上の歴史もあり、大暴落の後でも必ず回復し、いつの間にか高値を更新し続けている。そして2020年3月のコロナショックでは、わずか半年でコロナショック前の高値を更新し、回復力は驚きだ。2021年の米国の総人口は3億3291万人で、2050年になっても増え続け、総人口は3億7941万人と推計されている。米国は移民の国であり、結果、世界各国から米国に人が集まり、長期にわたる人口増加を支えていく。

　　自立した経済運営ができない日本。一人っ子政策の弊害がみえてきた中国。先進国経済の域に達するにはまだ時間を要するインド。イギリスのEU離脱など、欧州経済もさまざまな問題を抱えている。米国は、資産の安定性が非常に高い国である。最高値を更新し続けてきた米国株式市場の歴史のなかで、投資家に支払われた配当金やキャピタルゲインは、莫大な金額になる。結局、投資マネーは米国を目指すことになる。

Reading

2-14

The lessons from America's astonishing economic record

If there is one thing that Americans of all political stripes can agree on, it is that the economy is broken. Nearly four-fifths tell pollsters that their children will be worse off than they are, the most since the survey began in 1990, when only
5 about two-fifths were as gloomy.

Yet the anxiety obscures a stunning success story — one of enduring but underappreciated outperformance. America remains the world's richest, most productive and most innovative big economy.

2-15
10 In 1990 America accounted for a quarter of the world's output, at market exchange rates. Thirty years on, that share is almost unchanged, even as China has gained economic clout. America's dominance of the rich world is startling. Today it accounts for 58% of the g7's gdp, compared with
15 40% in 1990. Adjusted for purchasing power, only those in über-rich petrostates and financial hubs enjoy a higher income per person. Average incomes have grown much faster than in western Europe or Japan. Also adjusted for purchasing power, they exceed $50,000 in Mississippi, America's poorest state
20 — higher than in France.

The record is as impressive for many of the ingredients of growth. America has nearly a third more workers than in 1990, compared with a tenth in western Europe and Japan. And, perhaps surprisingly, more of them have graduate and
25 postgraduate degrees. True, Americans work more hours on average than Europeans and the Japanese. But they are significantly more productive than both.

American firms own more than a fifth of patents registered abroad, more than China and Germany put together. All of the
30 five biggest corporate sources of research and development (R&D) are American; in the past year they have spent $200bn.

lessons：教訓

stripes：色彩

worse off：暮らしが悪くなる

as gloomy：同じように悲観的だ《as は副詞》

anxiety：不安

underappreciated：価値が正しく評価されていない

outperformance：卓越した業績

innovative：革新的な

accounted for 〜：〜を占めた

market exchange rate：市場為替レート

clout：影響力

dominance：優位性

g7's：G7（主要7か国）の

gdp：GDP《国民総生産》

Adjusted for purchasing power：購買力調整後

über-rich：超富裕な

per person：一人当たり

firms：会社

patents：特許

research and development：研究開発

Consumers everywhere have benefited from their innovations in everything from the laptop and the iPhone to artificial-intelligence chatbots. Investors who put $100 into the s&p 500 in 1990 would have more than $2,000 today, four times what they would have earned had they invested elsewhere in the rich world.

One retort to this could be that Americans trade higher incomes for less generous safety-nets. America's spending on social benefits, as a share of gdp, is indeed a great deal stingier than other countries'. But those benefits have become more European and, as the economy has grown, they have grown even faster. Tax credits for workers and children have become more generous. Health insurance for the poorest has expanded, notably under President Barack Obama.

America has the benefit of a large consumer market over which to spread the costs of R&D, and a deep capital market from which to raise finance.

The size and the quality of the workforce matters, too. America was blessed with a younger population and a higher fertility rate than other rich countries. That may not be easily remedied elsewhere, but countries can at least take inspiration from America's high share of immigrants, who in 2021 made up 17% of its workforce, compared with less than 3% in ageing Japan.

The Economist, April 13, 2023

benefited from 〜：〜から恩恵を受けている

laptop：ノートパソコン

artificial-intelligence chatbots：AI チャットボット

s&p 500：スタンダード・アンド・プアーズ総合500種株価指数《ダウ・ジョーンズ工業株30種平均と共に代表的株価指数》

had they invested 〜：《if を使わない仮定法》

trade 〜 for …：〜と引き換えに…を得る

Tax credits：税額控除

raise finance：資金を調達する

fertility rate：出生率

take inspiration from 〜：〜に何かしら感じるものを得る

Exercises

Multiple Choice

次の1〜2の英文を完成させ、3〜5の英文の質問に答えるために、a〜dの中から最も適切なものを1つ選びなさい。

1. No matter what their political opinion is, Americans share the view that

   a. their economy is improving steadily.
   b. their economy is doing badly.
   c. their children will be wealthier than them.
   d. their children are less gloomy about the future than they are.

2. Between 1990 and now America's share of the G7's GDP has

   a. risen to 58%.
   b. risen by 58%.
   c. remained almost unchanged.
   d. fallen to 40%.

3. What percentage of the world's output did America account for in 1990?

   a. About 15%.
   b. About 25%.
   c. Over 35%.
   d. Over 45%.

4. How has the number of workers in America changed since 1990?

   a. It has decreased by a third.
   b. It has increased by a tenth.
   c. It has increased by almost a third.
   d. It has stayed constant.

5. How does America's spending on social benefits compare with other countries?

   a. It has grown, but more slowly than the economy.
   b. It has steadily declined.
   c. It is proportionately less than in Europe.
   d. It has become higher than in Europe.

本文の内容に合致するものにT（True）、合致しないものにF（False）をつけなさい。

(　　) **1.** America has a productive economy and young population.

(　　) **2.** The United States accounts for over half of global GDP.

(　　) **3.** Even the state of Mississippi has higher average purchasing power than France.

(　　) **4.** Americans work longer hours than the Japanese.

(　　) **5.** The writer admires America's success in keeping immigration low.

Vocabulary

次の１〜８の語句は、経済に関する反意語です。（　）内に最も適切な下のa〜hの語群、また［　］内に下のA〜Hの日本語句の説明に入れなさい。

1. devaluation ［　　　　］ ↔ （　　　　）［平価切上げ］
2. （　　　）market ［強気市場］ ↔ bear market ［　　　　］
3. inflationary spiral ［　　　］ ↔ （　　　）spiral ［デフレスパイラル］
4. yen's（　　　）［円安］ ↔ yen's appreciation ［　　　　］
5. credit（　　　）［金融引き締め］ ↔ credit relaxation ［　　　　］
6. trade deficit ［　　　］ ↔ trade（　　　）［貿易収支黒字］
7. economic（　　　）［不景気］ ↔ economic booming ［　　　　］
8. creditor country ［　　　　］ ↔ （　　　　）country ［債務国］

a. bull	**A.** インフレスパイラル
b. depreciation	**B.** 円高
c. debtor	**C.** 金融緩和
d. deflationary	**D.** 好景気
e. revaluation	**E.** 債権国
f. slumping	**F.** 平価切下げ
g. squeeze	**G.** 貿易収支赤字
h. surplus	**H.** 弱気市場

17

●インドは人口で中国を追い抜く　果たして経済では？

インド・ムンバイのダダール市場の人混み。インドは人口で中国を追い抜くが、果して、人口増加のメリットとデメリットは？

写真：Redux ／アフロ

Before you read

Republic of India
インド共和国

面積　3,287,590km²（日本の8.7倍）（世界７位）
人口　1,310,000,000人（世界２位）
首都　ニューデリー／デリー連邦直轄地
最大都市　ムンバイ
公用語　英語、ヒンズー語／識字率　75.6%
民族　インド・アーリア族　72%
　　　　ドラヴィダ族　25%／モンゴロイド族　３%
宗教　ヒンズー教　79.8%／イスラム教　14.2%
　　　　キリスト教　2.3%／シーク教　1.7%
　　　　仏教　0.7%／ジャイナ教　0.4%
GDP　２兆7,187億ドル（世界７位）
　　　　１人当たりGDP　2,038ドル（世界144位）
通貨　インド・ルビー／**政体**　共和制

Words and Phrases

次の１〜５の語の説明として最も近いものをａ〜ｅから１つ選び、（　）内に記入しなさい。

1. fanfare　　　　（　　）　　　**a.** high position
2. perch　　　　　（　　）　　　**b.** celebration
3. workforce　　　（　　）　　　**c.** people in work or available for work
4. hinder　　　　（　　）　　　**d.** not moving
5. stagnated　　　（　　）　　　**e.** impede progress

Summary

次の英文は記事の要約です。下の語群から最も適切な語を１つ選び、（　）内に記入しなさい。

2-19

Even as its population (　　　　) China's, India is expected to have the fastest-growing economy this year. And with economic growth (　　　) population growth, the pro-Hindu government is (　　　) Hindus to have more children. Yet the economy faces challenges such as unequal regional development and poor (　　　). Another problem is the relatively (　　　　) number of women in paid work.

encouraging　　exceeding　　infrastructure　　low　　surpasses

　　国連は、2023年４月19日、インドの人口が14億2860万人となり、中国を抜いて世界で最も多くなる見通しだと発表した。2023年７月１日時点の人口の推計では、インドが、中国の14億2570万人を290万人上回って、世界で最も多くなると報告している。国連は、インドの人口の推計では、2050年には16億6800万人に達する見通しを示している。乳幼児の死亡率が下がり続けることなどが背景にあるようだ。

　　2022年のインドの平均年齢は27.9歳だ。因みに日本は、48.7歳、中国38.5歳だ。インドの働く世代は、2021年の総人口の67.5％も占めた。モディ政権は、国内の製造業を推進し、国内に進出する企業に補助金を支給するなどして、雇用創出を図ってきた。豊富な労働力をいかした経済成長に期待がかかる一方、ごみが増えつづけ、下水処理施設の整備など衛生関連のインフラ整備などの課題も浮上している。

　　エジプト、エチオピア、ナイジェリア、タンザニア、コンゴ民主共和国、パキスタン、フィリピン、インドの８か国で今後人口が急増し、2050年までに予想される世界人口の増加の半分を占める見通しである一方、欧米や日本など世界の３分の２の人が暮らす地域では出生率が低い水準にとどまり、人口が増えていく地域と減っていく地域の二極化が進むと分析されている。

Reading

India Is Passing China in Population. Can Its Economy Ever Do the Same?

India's leaders rarely miss a chance to cheer the nation's many distinctions, from its status as the world's largest democracy to its new rank as the world's fifth-largest economy, after recently surpassing Britain, its former colonial overlord.

colonial overlord：植民地君主（旧宗主国）

5　Now, another milestone is approaching, though with no fanfare from Indian officials. The country will soon pass China in population, knocking it from its perch for the first time in at least three centuries, data released by the United Nations on Wednesday shows.

officials：当局者

perch：地位

10　India has a work force that is young and expanding even as those in most industrialized countries, including China, are aging and in some cases shrinking.

2-21

But India's immense size and lasting growth also lay bare its enormous challenges, renewing in this latest spotlight 15 moment a perennial, if still uncomfortable, question: When will it ever fulfill its vast promise and become a power on the order of China or the United States?

lay bare ～：～を露呈させる

perennial：多年にわたる

on the order of ～：～に匹敵する

India's infrastructure, while vastly improved from where it stood a few decades ago, remains far behind China's, 20 hindering foreign investment, which has stagnated in recent years. Another major problem is that only one in five Indian women are in the formal work force, among the lowest rates anywhere and one that has actually declined as India has gotten more prosperous. Apart from quashing the aspirations 25 of the country's hundreds of millions of young women, keeping them out of formal jobs acts as a terrible brake on the economy.

stagnated：停滞している

Apart from ～：～なことは別として

quashing ～：～を押し潰す

aspirations：願望

keeping ～ out of …：～を…から遠ざける

2-22

India's economy has been growing much faster than its population for a generation, and the proportion of Indians 30 living in extreme poverty has plummeted. Yet most Indians remain poor by global standards.

plummeted：急落している

The rate of development across the huge country remains widely unequal, with some Indian states akin to middle-income nations and others struggling to provide the basics.

35 When Gayathri Rajmurali, a local politician from the southern state of Tamil Nadu, found herself in India's north for the first time this year, the disparity shocked her. "The north, they are behind 10 to 15 years to our places," she said, pointing to indicators like basic infrastructure and average 40 income.

2-23

And then there is the combustible environment created by the Hindu-first nationalism of Prime Minister Narendra Modi's ruling party, as his support base has sped up a century-old campaign to reshape India's pluralist democratic tradition 45 and relegate Muslims and other minorities to second-class citizenship. Demographic numbers are part of the political provocation game, with right-wing leaders often falsely portraying India's Muslim population of 200 million as rising sharply in proportion to the Hindu population as they call on 50 Hindu families to have more children.

2-24
Among major economies, India's is projected to be the fastest-growing this year, with the World Bank expecting it to expand 6.3 percent in the new fiscal year after a sharp downturn early in the pandemic.

55 And India is increasingly looking to capitalize on China's economic and diplomatic difficulties to become a higher-end manufacturing alternative — it is now producing a small share of Apple's iPhones — and a sought-after geopolitical partner and counterweight.

Mujib Mashal and Alex Travelli
The New York Times, April 19, 2023

widely unequal：大いに一様ではない

akin to ~：～に似ている

found herself in ~：～を訪れた

disparity：格差

behind 10 to 15 years to ~：～と比べて10年から15年遅れている

indicators：指標

combustible：可燃性の

Hindu-first nationalism：ヒンズー至上国家主義

pluralist：多元主義の

relegate ~ to …：～を…に追いやる

Demographic：人口統計

provocation：挑発

World Bank：世界銀行《国際金融機関》

fiscal year：会計年度

downturn：景気後退

looking to ~：～することを模索する

capitalize on ~：～を利用する

alternative：（中国に）代わるもの

sought-after：人気の

geopolitical：地政学的

counterweight：対抗勢力

Exercises

次の1～2の英文の質問に答え、3～5の英文を完成させるために、a～dの中から最も適切なものを1つ選びなさい。

1. What proportion of Indian women are in the formal workforce?

    a. One in two.

    b. One in three.

    c. One in four.

    d. One in five.

2. How does Indian population growth compare with economic growth?

    a. The former has grown faster than the latter.

    b. The latter has grown faster than the former.

    c. Neither the economy nor the population has grown.

    d. The population is shrinking because of low economic growth.

3. According to the text, India is being challenged by having

    a. the most aging workforce in the world.

    b. a shrinking economy.

    c. a lack of infrastructure.

    d. all of the above problems.

4. According to the writer, India's Muslim population

    a. is rising sharply.

    b. cannot be said to be rising sharply.

    c. is falling sharply.

    d. has exceeded the Hindu population.

5. According to the politician from Tami Nadu,

    a. the north is better developed than the south.

    b. the south is better developed than the north.

    c. north Indian culture is shockingly different from south Indian culture.

    d. economic levels in the east are 10 to 15 times higher than in the west.

True or False

本文の内容に合致するものにT（True）、合致しないものにF（False）をつけなさい。

(   ) **1.** India exceeds China in population and economy.

(   ) **2.** India's economy has been growing faster than its population.

(   ) **3.** Indians' living standards have surpassed those of developed countries.

(   ) **4.** The Indian north surpasses the south in infrastructure.

(   ) **5.** Prime Minister Modi's party has focused mainly on helping Muslims.

Vocabulary

次の1〜6は、人口や経済、少子高齢化に関する社会問題を扱った英文です。日本文に合うように、下の語群から最も適切な語を1つ選び、（　）内に記入しなさい。

1. 人口の増加は深刻な社会問題を生んでいる。

Population (　　　　　　　) has given rise to serious social problems.

2. 国のインフラを維持するには、多くの資金が必要である。

More money is needed to (　　　　　　) the country's infrastructure.

3. あの国は、厳しい経済格差に直面している。

That country is confronted with severe economic (　　　　　　).

4. 日本社会が抱える問題に少子高齢化がある。

Problems facing Japan include the (　　　　　) birthrate and (　　　　　) society.

5. 社会保障制度を充実させる必要がある。

The social (　　　　　) system should be enhanced.

6. 国籍や性別、職業などで人を差別してはいけない。

Do not (　　　　　) against people based on nationality, gender or occupation.

| aging | declining | disparity | discriminate |
| growth | maintain | security | |

●イランが通貨危機に直面　その理由は？

イラン・テヘランのグランドバザール。イランは現在、通貨危機に直面しているが、果して、核開発を巡り米国による経済制裁だけが、その理由なのか？

写真：Redux／アフロ

Before you read

Islamic Republic of Iran
イラン・イスラム共和国

面積　1,648,195km²（世界17位・日本の約4.4倍）
人口　74,196,000人（世界18位）
首都　テヘラン
公用語　ペルシャ語
宗教　イスラム教・シーア派　90%／スンニ派　9%
民族　ペルシャ人　51%／アラブ人　4%
　　　トルコ系アゼルバイジャン人　25%
　　　クルド人　7%
識字率　85%
GDP　3,663億ドル（世界32位）
　　　1人当たり GDP　6,980米ドル
通貨　イラン・リアル
政体　立憲イスラム共和制

Words and Phrases

次の１〜５の語の説明として最も近いものを a 〜 e から１つ選び、（　）内に記入しなさい。

1. plunge	（　）		**a.**	drop sharply
2. convert	（　）		**b.**	complaint or problem
3. worthless	（　）		**c.**	get weaker or worse
4. dim	（　）		**d.**	having no value
5. grievance	（　）		**e.**	exchange

Summary

次の英文は記事の要約です。下の語群から最も適切な語を１つ選び、（　）内に記入しなさい。

2-25

Recent protests against (　　　　　) restrictions in Iran have been (　　　　　) by economic frustrations. Western sanctions, which aim to curb the country's development of nuclear (　　　　　), partly explain the economic disaster. But many Iranians also (　　　　　) government incompetence. As the people get increasingly (　　　　　), the government is cracking down with increasing violence.

blame	desperate	intensified	social	weapons

　イランの通貨イラン・リアルの対ドル為替レートの下落に歯止めがかからない。2022年８月半ばに１ドル＝約29万リアルだったが、下落を続け、12月末には40万リアルとなった。2023年に入っても下落の勢いは止まらず、１月28日には44万5,000リアルを記録し、５カ月半で約50％下落した計算になる。また、インフレ率は、2022年８月後半以降は徐々にではあるものの下降傾向にあったが、直近12月から１月の消費者物価指数上昇率は、総合が前年同月比51.3％、食品飲料が70.1％と、いずれも増加に転じている。

　昨年９月のジナ・マフサ・アミニ（22歳）の警察による拘束中の死亡に端を発する抗議行動と政権側からの厳しい弾圧が始まって以来、イラン通貨の価値を29％減じた。通貨安と高インフレの２重の打撃により、生活費危機がもたらされ、国民の不満が高まっている。ウクライナとの戦争を行っているロシアへの軍事的支援、EU によって準軍事組織のイラン革命防衛隊に対して最近課した制裁の厳しさ、2015年核合意の復活の不透明な展望により、イランが政治的な孤立を深め、その結果リアルの価値が下落したのだと確信されている。

Reading

2-26

Iran's Rulers, Shaken by Protests, Now Face Currency Crisis

Currency Crisis：通貨危機

As their currency plunged to new lows recently, Iranians did what they had grown all too used to: They crowded exchange shops, hoping to convert their increasingly worthless rials into dollars.

lows：安値

too used to：慣れ親しんだ

convert 〜 into …：〜を…に交換する

5　At the grocery store, prices had climbed so high that many people had only enough to buy vegetables. And as the Persian New Year approached, some had little left for holiday meals, shopping and travel.

Persian New Year：ノウルーズ《イランのヒジュラ暦による新年の祭日》

had little left for 〜：〜のための準備がほとんど出来なくなった

2-27

　The rial has lost some 30 percent of its value against
10　the dollar since the beginning of the year, the latest setback for an economy whose outlook has steadily dimmed since 2018, when President Donald J. Trump walked away from an agreement to limit Iran's nuclear activities in exchange for lifting sanctions.

walked away from 〜：〜から離脱した

in exchange for 〜：〜と引き換えに

lifting sanctions：制裁解除

added to 〜：〜を増大させた

15　The currency's recent decline has added to a sense of despair and to Iranians' grievances against the government. The prospects for economic relief and political change now appear slim: The nuclear deal looks unlikely to be revived, and a violent crackdown by the authorities has largely crushed the
20　mass protests against clerical rule that erupted in September.

crackdown：取締り

clerical rule：聖職者による支配

2-28

　Frustration with the theocratic rulers, whether over economic policies or social restrictions, also drove the recent protests, which posed one of the greatest challenges to the Islamic Republic since it was established in 1979.

theocratic：神権的な

Islamic Republic：イスラム共和国

25　Iran, its residents often say, should be rich, with some of the world's largest oil reserves and a well-educated population. Instead, with inflation routinely topping 50 percent annually, some Iranians can no longer afford meat.

reserves：埋蔵量

　Economic frustration over a sudden spike in gasoline
30　prices set off major protests in 2019. But last year's demonstrations, which began after the death in police custody

spike：高騰

set off 〜：〜を引き起こした

of 22-year-old Mahsa Amini, who was accused of violating the strict religious dress code for women, first took aim at the mandatory head scarf law and the systemic sexism protesters said it symbolized.

The movement quickly expanded, however, to encompass a broad range of grievances with the ruling establishment, including a lack of political and social freedoms, corruption and economic mismanagement.

Economists say the current crisis can be traced to years of Western sanctions on Iran's oil industry and financial sector over an Iranian nuclear program that the U.S. and its allies suspect is aimed at producing weapons.

But the government's handling of a series of recent crises did little to dispel the widely held belief that mismanagement and corruption are also to blame.

In the last several months, victims of an earthquake in northern Iran denounced a too-little-too-late emergency response, according to social media posts. The authorities responded to protests with water cannons.

Mohamed Ali Kadivar, a Boston College sociologist who studies Iranian protest movements, said that "because of the dominance of the hard liners, the people who take government jobs are loyal, they're not people with expertise," which makes the system "incapable of problem-solving."

Much of the economy is controlled by well-connected government loyalists or the powerful Iranian Revolutionary Guard Corps, creating advantages for insiders that, along with the political uncertainty, hinder investment.

Vivian Yee
The New York Times, March 6, 2023

accused of 〜：〜したと告発された
took aim at 〜：〜に狙いを定めた

encompass 〜：〜を網羅する

corruption：汚職

financial sector：金融部門

is aimed at 〜：〜することを目的としている《主語は program》

did little to 〜：〜にはほとんど役立たなかった
dispel 〜：〜を払しょくする

hard liners：強硬派

expertise：専門知識

Iranian Revolutionary Guard Corps：イラン革命防衛隊
creating advantages for 〜：〜に利益をもたらしている

Exercises

Multiple Choice

次の１〜３の英文の質問に答え、４〜５の英文を完成させるために、ａ〜ｄの中から最も適切なものを１つ選びなさい。

1. Why have Iranians been crowding exchange shops recently?

    a. To convert their rials into dollars.

    b. To exchange dollars for rials.

    c. To purchase goods with their rials.

    d. To protest against the declining currency value.

2. What event in 2018 contributed to Iran's economic crisis?

    a. A decline in oil prices.

    b. Economic sanctions by European countries.

    c. President Trump's withdrawal from a nuclear agreement.

    d. Political protests against the government.

3. According to the text, what triggered major protests in Iran in 2019?

    a. A spike in gasoline prices.

    b. The death of Mahsa Amini.

    c. Violation of the religious dress code.

    d. Corruption and economic mismanagement.

4. The recent mass protests have largely ended because of

    a. economic relief measures.

    b. a revival of the nuclear deal with America.

    c. a violent crackdown by Iranian authorities.

    d. international support for the protesters.

5. Investment in Iran's economy is hindered by

    a. political uncertainty and corruption.

    b. a lack of skilled and educated employees.

    c. the clothing rules imposed by religious leaders.

    d. the protests by Iranian women against their government.

True or False

本文の内容に合致するものにＴ（True）、合致しないものにＦ（False）をつけなさい。

(　　) **1.** The rial has gained some 20% in value against the U.S. dollar.

(　　) **2.** Iranians were disappointed with their government over economic policies.

(　　) **3.** Although Iran has among the world's highest oil reserves, some Iranians cannot eat meat anymore.

(　　) **4.** Iranians held demonstrations against their wage-push inflation.

(　　) **5.** Mahsa Amini was accused of breaking Iranian commercial law.

Vocabulary

次の１〜８は、「通貨」に関する英文です。下の語群の中から最も適切な語を１つ選び、(　　) 内に記入しなさい。

1. The (　　　　　) is the name of money used formerly in Italy and currently in Turkey.

2. One (　　　　) dollar is worth more than one New Zealand (　　　　).

3. Before adopting (　　　　) the Irish used pounds and the (　　　) used francs.

4. There are 100 centavos in one Brazilian (　　　　).

5. Danes, Norwegians and Swedes all use a version of the (　　　　).

6. Teachers in Iran are paid in (　　　　).

7. The (　　　　) refers to an old British coin and also to money used by Kenyans now.

8. Argentinians, Mexicans and Filipinos all call their currency the (　　　　).

Australian	dollar	euros	French	krone
lira	peso	real	rial	shilling

- 「寿司テロ」により、回転寿司のレーンが停止
- 大阪の「飲食店テロ」で2人逮捕

「寿司テロ」や「飲食店テロ」が勃発。自己顕示欲の発露か、それとも単なる…？

写真：アフロ

Before you read

Questions

1. What do you think of sushi terrorism?

   「寿司テロ」についてどう思いますか？

2. Has sushi terrorism changed your eating out behavior?

   寿司テロであなたの外食に対する態度は変わりましたか？

次の１〜５の語の説明として最も近いものをａ〜ｅから１つ選び、（　）内に記入しなさい。

1. reputation　（　）　　**a.** rush

2. tamper　（　）　　**b.** not clean

3. unhygienic　（　）　　**c.** interfere with or manipulate

4. scramble　（　）　　**d.** image of a company or person

5. condiment　（　）　　**e.** food addition, such as sauce or spice

Summary

次の英文は記事の要約です。下の語群から最も適切な語を１つ選び、（　）内に記入しなさい。

2-31　Following a series of viral videos showing (　　　　　) acts by customers, revolving sushi restaurants are desperate to win (　　　　　) business. Choshimaru has (　　　　　) off the conveyor belts at all of its restaurants. Sushiro has introduced (　　　　　) via touch-screen devices. Other food businesses have also been affected. Recently, two men were arrested after filming their own antisocial (　　　　　) at Yoshinoya.

back　　behavior　　ordering　　switched　　unhygienic

　回転寿司店での迷惑行為の動画が SNS 上に拡散した問題で、回転寿司店が警察に被害届を提出し、受理された。警察は、威力業務妨害などの疑いで迷惑行為をした高校生や動画を撮影、投稿した人物の事情聴取をした。問題が発覚したのは2023年２月中旬。「はま寿司」の店舗で、男子高校生が、ガリの容器に直接、箸を入れて食べる行為の動画が SNS 上に拡散した。この動画の拡散前の１月には、「スシロー」で男性客が備え付けのしょうゆボトルや湯飲みをなめる動画が広められた。また２月には「くら寿司」で、男性客がしょうゆ差しを口につける動画が SNS 上に投稿された。「はま寿司」の別の店でも、男性客がほかの客が注文したすしの上にわさびをのせる動画が拡散した。

　いずれのケースもその後、動画に映っていた本人と撮影と投稿をした人物が逮捕されるなど刑事事件に発展している。はま寿司の広報は「お客さまを不安にさせる行為にはしっかりと対応していく」としている。回転寿司チェーンの中には、不正行為を検知するシステムを導入するなど、迷惑行為に対して新たな設備投資を迫られるケースもある。動画を投稿した人物が「面白いと思ったから」と供述している気軽な動機が"犯罪行為"にもなることを十分認識する必要がある。

Reading

2-32

'Sushi terrorism' sees Japan's conveyor belt restaurants grind to a halt

grind to a halt：きしみなが
ら停止する

In the weeks since a viral video appeared showing a teenager licking the open top of a communal soy sauce bottle and rubbing saliva on passing food at a *kaitenzushi* (conveyor belt sushi) restaurant, chains have scrambled to restore their
5 reputation for cleanliness — even if it means removing their main attraction.

viral：バイラル、口コミ

communal：共用の

rubbing saliva on ～：～
に唾液をこすりつける

scrambled to ～：～しよう
と躍起になる

Choshimaru, which operates restaurants in the greater Tokyo area, recently said its conveyor belts would grind to a halt, forcing staff to deliver orders by hand, after a video
10 showed a diner placing a cigarette butt in a container of pickled ginger.

Choshimaru：銚子丸《企業
名》

operates ～：～を運営する

greater Tokyo area：首都
圏

diner：食事客

2-33

In response, staff at the chain started taking condiments and utensils to tables every time a new group of diners took their seats.

condiments：調味料

15 But then Choshimaru went a step further and announced that, for the time being, conveyor belts at all 63 of its restaurants would be switched off, with customers forced to wait for staff to bring their orders directly to the table.

for the time being：当分の
間

The kaitenzushi industry, worth an estimated ¥740bn
20 (£4.5bn/$5.4bn) in 2021, has been hit hard by the spate of viral videos showing, among other misdemeanours, customers licking communal sauce bottles, daubing wasabi on food as it passes by, spraying sushi with hand sanitiser and snatching plates of food destined for other tables.

worth ～：～する価値があ
る

misdemeanours：軽犯罪

hand sanitiser：手指消毒液

destined for ～：～に送ら
れる予定の

2-34

25 The incidents have sent shares plummeting at Sushiro, the industry leader, and prompted operators to rethink how they serve their dishes.

shares plummeting：株価の
急落

Sushiro：スシロー《企業名》

Sushiro said last month that its sushi would be delivered only via an "express lane" to customers who order via touch-
30 screen devices, making it harder for other diners to tamper with food.

touch-screen devices：タッ
チパネル

The change came after Sushiro suffered a slump in customers, as more people shunned the convenience and novelty of kaitenzushi amid widespread media coverage of
35 "terrorism" targeting items of food.

The contagion has spread to other parts of Japan's budget restaurant sector. Gyoza no Osho, a popular chain of Chinese restaurants, has removed soy sauce and other condiments from tables — they are still available on request from staff —
40 while the ramen chain Ichiran has removed glasses from its counters and tables.

The Guardian, March 7, 2023

suffered a slump in customers：客足が低迷した

shunned 〜：〜を敬遠した

novelty：目新しさ

coverage：報道

contagion：伝染

budget：低予算の

Gyoza no Osho：餃子の王将《企業名》

on request：頼めば

Ichiran：一蘭《企業名》

Two arrested over video of unhygienic acts at Osaka restaurant

unhygienic：不衛生な

KYODO. Osaka — Two men have been arrested for allegedly
45 harming the business of Japanese beef bowl chain Yoshinoya with a video of one of them eating directly from a container of toppings meant for all customers, Osaka police said Tuesday.

R.S.*, 35, and T.O.*, 34, are also suspected of damaging property after a Yoshinoya restaurant in Osaka was forced to
50 discard red pickled ginger toppings and sanitize its containers.

According to the police, on Sept. 19, R.S. used chopsticks that he had eaten with to take some toppings from a container that he then ate, while T.O. filmed him on a smartphone. The footage was posted on social media and shared widely among
55 users.

The arrests of the two men come at a time when the country's major chains including revolving sushi restaurants are fighting to protect their businesses from videos of unhygienic behavior that are being shared widely online.

The Japan Times (Kyodo), April 4, 2023

Yoshinoya：吉野家《企業名》

＊共同通信社の指示に従い、名前表記を変更

damaging property：物的損害

Exercises

Multiple Choice

次の１～３の英文の質問に答え、４～５の英文を完成させるために、ａ～ｄの中から最も適切なものを１つ選びなさい。

1. What did Choshimaru recently announce about their conveyor belts?

   a. They would be replaced with new ones.

   b. They would be turned off at all their restaurants.

   c. They would be cleaned more frequently.

   d. They would be speeded up into express lanes.

2. How has Sushiro changed the way it serves sushi?

   a. It has asked customers to order via touch screens.

   b. It wants customers to rethink how they deliver food.

   c. It has forbidden customers from touching anything.

   d. It is only delivering orders directly to homes.

3. How have acts of 'terrorism' affected business?

   a. Entertaining videos have encouraged more people to go out to eat.

   b. Restaurants have had to spend over ¥70bn on new equipment.

   c. At least one sushi chain saw its share prices fall in value.

   d. Many beef bowl chains have had to close.

4. The Chinese restaurant mentioned in the article has

   a. started using disposable plates and chopsticks.

   b. been spraying its dishes with hand sanitizer.

   c. removed condiments such as soy sauce from tables.

   d. added extra soy sauce to food so that customers do not ask for it.

5. The men arrested in Osaka harmed one of Yoshinoya's restaurants by

   a. criticizing it in a video posted online.

   b. stealing items from the restaurant.

   c. forcing the restaurant to throw away toppings.

   d. causing it to turn off its conveyor belt for eight hours.

本文の内容に合致するものに T （True）、合致しないものに F （False）をつけなさい。

(   ) **1.** After a teenager was seen rubbing saliva on food, revolving sushi bar chains tried to restore their reputation for hygiene.

(   ) **2.** Choshimaru serves customers who touch a screen to order.

(   ) **3.** 'Sushi terrorism' has spread to other types of restaurant in Japan.

(   ) **4.** Yoshinoya runs a mutton bowl restaurant chain.

(   ) **5.** T.O. was arrested for doing damage to a Yoshinoya in Osaka.

Vocabulary

次の１〜８は、「how to eat sushi properly」に関する英文です。適切な語を下の語群から１つ選び、（   ）内に記入しなさい。

1. If you are interested in watching your food preparation or (   ) with the sushi chef, ask to be seated at the sushi (   ).

2. You may be offered a hot wet (   ) called oshibori, so use it to (   ) your hands.

3. It is OK to eat sushi with your (   ).

4. Don't put wasabi (   ) into the shoyu dish. Sushi comes with wasabi placed (   ) the fish by the sushi chef.

5. Pick up the sushi and (   ) the fish into your soy sauce.

6. Eat sushi in one (   ).

7. Ginger is considered a palate (   ) and eaten between bites or different types of sushi.

8. It is (   ) to thank the sushi chef if you were seated at the sushi bar.

bite	cleanser	conversing	counter	dip	directly
hands	polite	towel	under	wash	

Unit 20

●中南米のコカイン・カルテルと欧州

オランダ・ロッテルダム港で荷物検査の訓練をする麻薬探知犬。
麻薬の「ヨーロッパ市場」を巡る、水際での攻防

写真：AFP ／アフロ

Before you read

Plurinational State of Bolivia
ボリビア多民族国

面積　1,100,000km²（日本の約３倍）／**首都**　ラパス
人口　11,510,000人／**民族**　先住民　41%　非先住民　59%
公用語　スペイン語・ケチュア語
宗教　キリスト教・カトリック　95%
GDP　389億3,500万ドル
　　　１人当たりの GDP　3,321ドル
通貨　ボリビアーノス／**政体**　立憲共和制／**識字率**　81%

Republic of Colombia
コロンビア共和国

面積　1,139,000km²（日本の約３倍）／**首都**　ボゴタ
人口　51,270,000人／**民族**　混血　75%　ヨーロッパ系　20%
公用語　スペイン語／**宗教**　キリスト教・カトリック　90%
GDP　3,143億ドル／１人当たりの GDP　6,160ドル
通貨　ペソ／**政体**　立憲共和制／**識字率**　95.6%

Republic of Peru
ペルー共和国

面積　1,290,000km²（日本の約3.4倍）／**首都**　リマ
人口　32,970,000人
民族　混血　60%　先住民　26%　白人系　6%　アフリカ系　4%
公用語　スペイン語
宗教　キリスト教・カトリック　81%／プロテスタント　13%
GDP　2,020億ドル／１人当たりの GDP　6,127ドル
通貨　ソル／**政体**　立憲共和制／**識字率**　94.5%

次の1～5の語句の説明として最も近いものをa～eから1つ選び、（　）内に記入しなさい。

1. lucrative　　（　　）　　a. criminal organization
2. flood　　　　（　　）　　b. fill or overwhelm
3. extract　　　（　　）　　c. profitable
4. upside down　（　　）　　d. reversed or completely changed
5. syndicate　　（　　）　　e. derive

Summary

次の英文は記事の要約です。下の語群から最も適切な語を1つ選び、（　）内に記入しなさい。

2-37

　Drug cartels are (　　　　) Europeans' surging demand for cocaine, with dealers (　　　　) the drug as easily as pizza. The (　　　　) trade may have helped some South American farmers more than their governments have. But the main (　　　　) go to Mexican, Moroccan, Albanian, Serbian, Kosovan and Italian gangs. They are not afraid to (　　　　) the police or use violence.

bribe　　delivering　　exploiting　　illegal　　profits

　　北米やヨーロッパのコカイン市場が南米コロンビアやペルー、ボリビアの熱帯雨林破壊に拍車をかけている。研究者や議員、環境保護活動家が数十年にわたり警告を続けてきたが、国連薬物犯罪事務所によると、2010年にはコロンビアだけで6万2000ヘクタールがコカ栽培に利用されたと推定されている。栽培用に土地が開墾され周辺地域の生活が潤っているが、森林破壊が進む。コカ栽培には、有害な殺虫剤や殺菌剤、肥料が使われ、その一部は石油を原料としている。ペースト状にすり潰したコカの葉を、ガソリンや灯油などの石油製品に浸して抽出する工程はコカイン精製の常套手段だ。密売コカインの製造には、1キロあたり80リットルの灯油が使用される。
　　2022年11月には、スペイン、フランス、ベルギー、オランダとアラブ首長国連邦の5か国で大量のコカインが押収された。容疑者らによるコカインの欧州への密輸の規模は膨大で、売買には暗号化された通信手段が用いられている。今回の捜査で押収したコカイン33トンは、末端価格23億5000万ドル（約3250億円）に相当する。欧州での末端価格は高く、南米のカルテルには非常に魅力的だ。コロンビアから船で密輸されたコカインの多くは、パナマやメキシコの港でコンテナに積み込まれ、北欧に向け出荷される。ブラジルの港は、ボリビアのコカインの輸出の中心地になっており、欧州向けのコンテナに積み込まれるという。

Reading

Latin American cocaine cartels bring violence to Europe

Paris — "Seventy euros for one, 120 for two," said the cocaine dealer as the young woman opened her door on Paris' chic Left Bank.

"I'm like all the delivery riders speeding around Paris
5 dropping off sushi and groceries," he smiled.

Getting cocaine in many of Europe's big cities is now as easy as ordering a pizza.

Twenty or so minutes after you place your order by WhatsApp or Signal, a dealer can be at your door.

10 Europe has become one of the most lucrative markets for big drug cartels, who have not hesitated about using the corruption and extreme violence that has served them so well in South America.

The cocaine flooding Europe begins its journey in the high
15 mountain plateaus of Bolivia, Colombia and Peru, where the coca leaves from which the drug is extracted are grown.

In Catatumbo in northeast Colombia, Jose del Carmen Abril relies on coca to feed his eight children.

"Coca … has replaced the government which was never
20 very present here," said the 53-year-old. "It has helped us build schools, health centers, roads and houses."

Despite the billions spent over the decades by Washington and Bogota in their "war on drugs," peasants continue to grow more and more coca, with harvests up 14% in 2021 to an all-
25 time high of 1,400 tons, according to the United Nations.

Colombia supplies two-thirds of the world's cocaine. But the fall of the Cali and Medellin cartels in the 1990s, and the peace deal signed in 2016 with the Marxist FARC guerrillas, turned the trade upside down.

30 Once mere middlemen, the Mexican cartels have since taken almost total control of the market, from financing

---

cartels：カルテル（組織連合）

dealer：売人

chic：シックな、スマートな

Left Bank：セーヌ川左岸地区

dropping off 〜：〜を届ける

WhatsApp：《アプリ名》

Signal：《アプリ名》

drug：薬物

corruption：腐敗、汚職

flooding 〜：〜に氾濫する

extracted：抽出される

replaced 〜：〜に取って代わった

Bogota：ボゴタ《コロンビアの首都、同国政府の意》

an all-time high of 〜：史上最高の〜

peace deal：和平協定

FARC：コロンビア革命軍

turned 〜 upside down：〜をひどく混乱させた

middlemen：仲介業者

---

118 Unit 20

2-41

production to supervising cocaine smuggling.

The Sinaloa and Jalisco cartels at first concentrated on their "natural" market, the United States, before switching their
35 focus to Europe, where cocaine consumption has exploded.

The traffickers follow a well-trodden "business plan," with Mexican cartels selling to European multinational crime syndicates, sometimes via fixers who divide up the cargos to spread the costs and risks.

40 The Moroccan "Mocro mafia" in Belgium and the Netherlands, Albanian, Serb or Kosovan mafia and the Calabrian Ndrangheta divide up the market according to their territories and specializations.

2-42

A kilogram of cocaine bought for $1,000 in South America
45 can be sold for €35,000 in Europe. Once out of the port and cut with other substances, it will then be sold on to customers for €70 a gram, its value having gone up close to a hundredfold by the time it hits the street.

Such enormous profits allow a huge war chest to buy off
50 dockers, cargo agents, truckers, and sometimes customs and police officers, to get cocaine out of the ports.

As well as buying complicity and silence, the huge sums to be made have fueled extreme violence in northern Europe's port cities.

55 Antwerp — the main gateway of illegal drugs into Europe — has recorded more than 200 drug-linked violent incidents in the last five years, with an 11-year-old girl killed last week after bullets were fired into a house in the Merksem residential district.

Laetitia Drevet, Arthur Connan, Philippel Alfroy, Julie Capelle and David Salazar
The Japan Times (AFP-JIJI), January 23, 2023

---

supervising cocaine smuggling：コカイン密輸の監督

Calabrian：カラブリア州の《イタリア半島のつま先部分の州名》

Ndrangheta：「ンドランゲタ」《マフィア名で、世界で最も強力な組織犯罪集団と見なされる》

specializations：専門性

cut with ～：～と分離され

it hits the street：通りに出回る

war chest：軍資金

buy off ～：～を買収する

dockers：港湾労働者

customs：税関

complicity：共謀

Antwerp：アントワープ《ベルギー北部の港湾都市》

residential district：住宅地区

Exercises

Multiple Choice

次の１～２の英文の質問に答え、３～５の英文を完成させるために、ａ～ｄの中から最も適切なものを１つ選びなさい。

1. Why is buying cocaine compared to ordering pizzas?

    a. Europeans can have it brought to their doors easily.

    b. It has become almost as cheap as an Italian meal.

    c. Pizza companies are delivering it alongside food.

    d. Sales are controlled by the Italian mafia.

2. What has contributed to the growth of coca cultivation in Colombia?

    a. Government support for farmers.

    b. Falling demand for cocaine in the United States.

    c. Farmers' reliance on coca for economic survival.

    d. International efforts to eradicate coca plants.

3. The chief port of entry for illegal drugs into Europe is

    a. Brussels.

    b. Paris.

    c. Antwerp.

    d. Amsterdam.

4. Between its origin in South America and its sale in Europe cocaine increases

    a. by about 100% in value.

    b. nearly ten times in value.

    c. in value around a hundred times.

    d. in value 35,000 times.

5. The enormous profits to be made from cocaine have

    a. persuaded the Colombian and U.S. governments to legalize it.

    b. financed new schools and health centers in Europe.

    c. enabled Colombian farmers to take total control of the market.

    d. encouraged gangs in Europe to employ extreme violence.

本文の内容に合致するものにT（True）、合致しないものにF（False）をつけなさい。

(   ) **1.** In many European cities cocaine can be easily ordered by WhatsApp.

(   ) **2.** Some coca leaves have been grown in Bolivia.

(   ) **3.** Jose del Carmen Abril depends on his children heavily to live well.

(   ) **4.** A kilogram of cocaine in South America can be sold at fifty times the original price in Europe.

(   ) **5.** The Mexican cartels have taken over Medellin cartels and control the coca market.

Vocabulary

次の１〜８は、「持ち運ぶ」に関する英文です。日本文に合うように、【bring, carry, take】から１つ選び、必要があれば適当な形に直して記入しなさい。

1. 怪我をした少年は、救急車に運ばれた。
The injured boy was (   ) to the ambulance.

2. 手ぶらでパーティに来てください。
(   ) yourself to the party.

3. どうしてここに来たの？
What (   ) you here?

4. 電車で東京へ行った。
I (   ) a train to Tokyo.

5. いつも身分証明書を持っている。
I always (   ) my identity card about with me.

6. 毎朝犬を散歩に連れて行くのに慣れた。
I got used to (   ) the dog for a walk every morning.

7. 自分の仕事に誇りを持つべきだ。
You should (   ) pride in your work.

8. その冬は何度か大雪が降った。
The winter (   ) heavy snowfalls.

Unit 21

●ベートーヴェンの遺髪を DNA 検査　その結果は？

ベートーヴェンの遺髪を DNA 検査したら、死因や、
彼自身も知らない秘密が解明か？　　提供：アフロ

Before you read

Federal Republic of Germany
ドイツ連邦共和国

面積　357,578km²（日本の約94%）（世界63位）
人口　84,270,625人（世界18位）
民族　ゲルマン系ドイツ民族　80%
首都　ベルリン
公用語　ドイツ語
宗教　キリスト教・カトリック　30%
　　　キリスト教・ドイツ福音主義　30%
　　　イスラム教　5%／仏教　0.4%／ユダヤ教　0.3%
　　　ヒンズー教　0.1%／無宗教　34.1%
GDP　3兆8,433億3,500万ドル
　　　1人当たりのGDP　4万6,216ドル
通貨　ユーロ
政体　共和制
識字率　99%

次の１〜５の語の説明として最も近いものをa〜eから１つ選び、（　）内に記入しなさい。

1. abdominal　　（　　）　　　**a.** fine, narrow piece

2. jaundiced　　（　　）　　　**b.** inclined or prone

3. acolyte　　　（　　）　　　**c.** stomach-related

4. predisposed　（　　）　　　**d.** having yellowish discoloration

5. strand　　　　（　　）　　　**e.** follower

Summary

次の英文は記事の要約です。下の語群から最も適切な語を１つ選び、（　）内に記入しなさい。

2-43　　An analysis of (　　　　　　) of Beethoven's hair found DNA predisposing him to hepatitis B. This could have (　　　　　　) to his cirrhosis of the liver. The study also revealed that he was not (　　　　　) related to others in his family, suggesting an out-of-wedlock (　　　　　　) in his paternal line. The analysis offered no explanation for the composer's (　　　　) loss.

affair	genetically	hearing	led	strands

　　ルートヴィヒ・ファン・ベートーヴェン Ludwig van Beethoven は、1770年12月16日頃誕生し、1827年３月26日に生涯を閉じた。ドイツの作曲家、ピアニスト。音楽史において極めて重要な作曲家の一人であり、日本では「楽聖」とも呼ばれる。その作品は古典派音楽の集大成かつロマン派音楽の先駆とされ、後世の音楽家たちに多大な影響を与えた。

　　ベートーヴェンは、進行性の難聴のほか、慢性的な腹痛や下痢にも悩まされた。また晩年には大量に飲酒していたと伝えられている。死後に行われた解剖では肝臓、腎臓、脾臓のほか、多くの内臓に損傷が見られた。2023年、ケンブリッジ大学やドイツ・マックス・プランク人類史科学研究所などの国際研究チームにより毛髪のゲノム（全遺伝情報）解析が行われ、ベートーヴェンは死の１か月前にB型肝炎に感染しており、遺伝的に肝臓病になりやすい体質であったことが判明した。近年、ベートーヴェンの毛髪から通常の100倍近い鉛が検出されて注目を集めた。鉛は聴覚や精神状態に悪影響を与える重金属である。しかし、難聴の遺伝的原因は特定できなかった。

Reading

DNA From Beethoven's Hair Unlocks Medical and Family Secrets

It was March 1827 and Ludwig van Beethoven was dying. As he lay in bed, wracked with abdominal pain and jaundiced, grieving friends and acquaintances came to visit. And some asked a favor: Could they clip a lock of his hair for
5 remembrance?

Now, an analysis of strands of his hair has upended long held beliefs about his health.

The paper, by an international group of researchers, was published Wednesday in the journal Current Biology.

10 The detective work to solve the mysteries of Beethoven's illness began on Dec. 1, 1994, when a lock of hair said to be Beethoven's was auctioned by Sotheby's.

The story was that it was clipped by Ferdinand Hiller, a 15-year-old composer and ardent acolyte who visited
15 Beethoven four times before he died.

An analysis of the hair at Argonne National Laboratory in Illinois found lead levels as high as 100 times normal.

In 2007, authors of a paper in The Beethoven Journal, a scholarly journal published by San Jose State, speculated
20 that the composer might have been inadvertently poisoned by medicine, wine, or eating and drinking utensils.

That was where matters stood until 2014 when Tristan Begg, then a masters student studying archaeology at the University of Tübingen in Germany, realized that science had
25 advanced enough for DNA analysis using locks of Beethoven's hair.

William Meredith, a Beethoven scholar, began searching for other locks of Beethoven's hair, buying them with financial support from the American Beethoven Society, at private sales
30 and auctions.

First, the researchers tested the Hiller lock. Because it

DNA：デオキシリボ核酸

Unlocks 〜：〜を明かす《頭髪の lock とかけている》

wracked with 〜：〜に苦しんでいた
abdominal pain：腹痛
jaundiced：黄疸に罹っていた
asked a favor：お願いした
clip 〜：〜を切り取る
strands：（髪の毛の）房

ardent acolyte：熱心な信奉者

Argonne National Laboratory：アルゴンヌ国立研究所

San Jose State：サンノゼ州立大学
inadvertently poisoned：不注意に毒殺された

archaeology：考古学

American Beethoven Society：アメリカ・ベートーヴェン協会
private sales：相対売買

turned out to be from a woman, it was not — could not be — Beethoven's.

As for the other seven locks, one was inauthentic, five had
35 identical DNA and one could not be tested. The five locks with identical DNA were of different provenances and two had impeccable chains of custody, which gave the researchers confidence that they were hair from Beethoven.

2-47

When the group had the DNA sequence from Beethoven's
40 hair, they tried to answer longstanding questions about his health. For instance, why might he have died from cirrhosis of the liver?

He had DNA variants that made him genetically predisposed to liver disease. In addition, his hair contained traces of hepatitis
45 B DNA, indicating an infection with this virus, which can destroy a person's liver.

2-48

The composer could have been infected with hepatitis B during childbirth. In about a quarter of people, chronic infection will eventually lead to cirrhosis of the liver or liver cancer.

50 The study also revealed that Beethoven was not genetically related to others in his family line. His Y chromosome DNA differed from that of a group of five people with the same last name — van Beethoven — living in Belgium today and who, according to archival records, share a 16th-century ancestor
55 with the composer. That indicates there must have been an out-of-wedlock affair in Beethoven's direct paternal line.

The DNA analysis also offered no explanation for Beethoven's hearing loss, which started in his mid-20s and resulted in deafness in the last decade of his life.

Gina Kolata
The New York Times, March 22, 2023

As for 〜：〜については

inauthentic：本物ではない

identical：同一の

impeccable：非の打ちどころのない

custody：監理

confidence：確信

sequence：配列

cirrhosis of the liver：肝硬変

variants：変異

predisposed to 〜：〜に罹りやすい

traces of 〜：数量の〜

hepatitis B：Ｂ型肝炎

infection with 〜：〜に感染していること

chronic：慢性の

Y chromosome：Ｙ染色体

archival records：記録資料

out-of-wedlock affair：婚外関係

direct paternal line：直系父系

hearing loss：難聴

Exercises

次の１〜２の英文を完成させ、３〜５の英文の質問に答えるために、ａ〜ｄの中から最も適切なものを１つ選びなさい。

1. Some people thought Beethoven had died from poisoning because

    a. he took too much medicine.

    b. he tended to drink too much wine and eat too much food.

    c. high levels of lead were found in a hair sample.

    d. DNA taken from his ancestors showed traces of poison.

2. Researchers believe that some of the hair samples are Beethoven's as

    a. they were collected in the same place.

    b. they were collected by the same person.

    c. they share DNA despite coming from different places.

    d. they are owned by the American Beethoven Society.

3. Why is the poisoning theory unconvincing now?

    a. The hair that was analyzed was not his.

    b. Upon rechecking, the hair showed no indication of poisoning.

    c. Hiller had lied about the hair when he sold it to Sotheby's.

    d. DNA proved the composer was not related to Belgians sharing his name.

4. In which publication did the 2023 paper appear?

    a. In San Jose State Journal.

    b. In Current Biology.

    c. In the Argonne National.

    d. In The Beethoven Journal.

5. Why do the samples suggest the composer died of liver disease?

    a. They show that liver failure led to his deafness.

    b. They confirm that he was infected with hepatitis by his mother.

    c. Tests indicate that he probably had hepatitis B.

    d. Tests on the van Beethoven family in Belgium also showed liver disease.

True or False

本文の内容に合致するものにT（True）、合致しないものにF（False）をつけなさい。

(　　) **1.** San Jose State Journal in 2007 assumed that Beethoven might have been poisoned by medicine or wine.

(　　) **2.** Beethoven's hair showed traces of kidney cancer.

(　　) **3.** Beethoven had DNA variants that made him genetically inclined to hearing loss.

(　　) **4.** The article suggests Beethoven may have been infected with hepatitis B as a youth.

(　　) **5.** Argonne National Laboratory in Illinois found high levels of lead in Beethoven's hair.

Vocabulary

次のa～rの身体の内臓や部位に該当するものをイラストの1～18の中から選びなさい。

a.	anus	肛門	(	)
b.	bladder	膀胱	(	)
c.	diaphragm	横隔膜	(	)
d.	duodenum	十二指腸	(	)
e.	esophagus	食道	(	)
f.	gall bladder	胆嚢	(	)
g.	heart	心臓	(	)
h.	kidneys	腎臓	(	)
i.	large intestine	大腸	(	)
j.	liver	肝臓	(	)
k.	lungs	肺臓	(	)
l.	ovary	卵巣	(	)
m.	pancreas	膵臓	(	)
n.	rectum	直腸	(	)
o.	small intestine	小腸	(	)
p.	spleen	脾臓	(	)
q.	stomach	胃	(	)
r.	womb	子宮	(	)

Unit **22**

●レバノンでサマータイムを巡り大混乱

レバノン・ベイルートで、レバノン在住のイスラム教徒所有の時計と携帯電話での
現在の時刻が異なる。多宗教国家で、政治が不安定なレバノンの苦悩でもある

写真：ロイター／アフロ

Before you read

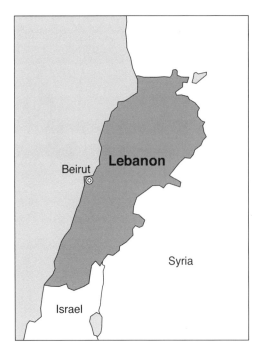

Lebanese Republic
レバノン共和国
1943年フランスより独立

面積　10,452km²（岐阜県とほぼ同じ）（世界161位）
首都・最大都市　ベイルート
公用語　アラビア語（フランス語と英語も通用）
人口　6,860,000人（世界107位）
民族　アラブ人　95%
　　　アルメニア人　4％
宗教　キリスト教（マロン派／ギリシャ正教
　　　ギリシャ・カトリック／ローマ・カトリック／
　　　アルメニア正教）40.4%
　　　イスラム教　54%
　　　ドゥルーズ派　5.6%
識字率　87.4%
GDP　534億ドル（世界87位）
　　　1人当たりのGDP　7,784ドル（世界99位）
通貨　レバノン・ポンド

次の１～５の語句の説明として最も近いものをａ～ｅから１つ選び、（　　）内に記入しなさい。

1. delayed	（　　）	**a.**	divisive or preferring one group
2. unilateral	（　　）	**b.**	order or law
3. skew	（　　）	**c.**	one-sided
4. sectarian	（　　）	**d.**	postponed
5. decree	（　　）	**e.**	lean toward or favor

Summary

次の英文は記事の要約です。下の語群から最も適切な語を１つ選び、（　　）内に記入しなさい。

2-49

When its government delayed the annual switch to DST this spring, it resulted in (　　　　) throughout Lebanon. Some institutions changed their (　　　　) while others did not. The delay was (　　　　) to benefit the Muslim majority, who were still observing Ramadan. But it (　　　　) tensions with the large Christian minority. It also added to the existing (　　　　) crisis.

clocks　　confusion　　economic　　increased　　intended

　　レバノン政府が土壇場でサマータイムの開始をラマダンの終わりまで１か月遅らせるという決定を下したことで、３月26日日曜日に大混乱が生じた。変更を実施する機関もあれば、拒否する機関もあり、多くのレバノン人は、同じ小さな国で、異なるタイムゾーンで仕事と学校のスケジュールを調整しなければならなかった。

　　イスラム教とキリスト教の宗派間の性質を帯び、マロン派を含む多くのキリスト教徒の政治家や機関がこの動きを拒否した。ほとんどのヨーロッパ諸国と同様に、レバノンも通常、３月の最終日曜日に時計を１時間進める。しかし３月23日の木曜日に、レバノン政府は、夏時間の開始を４月21日まで延期する決定を発表した。サマータイムの実施を延期することで、イスラム教徒がラマダンの断食を１時間早く破らないですむように求めた。しかし、一部のイスラム教徒は、断食は時間帯に関係なく夜明けに始まり、日没に終わるはずだと指摘した。

　　この問題を国の経済的・政治的問題から気を逸らそうとしているとも言われている。レバノンは、史上最悪の金融危機の真っただ中にあり、人口の４分の３が貧困の中で暮らし、何も対策を講じなければハイパーインフレに向かう可能性があると警告されている。

2-50

How did Lebanon end up with two rival time zones?
The chaotic switch to daylight savings time is emblematic of the country's politics

WHAT'S THE TIME in Lebanon? Until March 29th the answer will largely depend on your religion. On March 26th the country would normally have set its clocks forward to daylight saving time (DST), as is the custom on the final
5 Sunday of March. But at the last minute the government delayed the change. State institutions stayed on winter time, while church organisations and some schools and news outlets jumped an hour ahead. The result was a calendar nightmare. On March 27th Najib Mikati, the caretaker prime minister,
10 said that, following a cabinet vote, clocks would move forward after all, albeit three days late. Why did Lebanon end up so confused about the time of day?

2-51

On March 23rd Mr. Mikati announced that the switch to DST would be moved from March 26th to April 21st. He
15 gave no reason for the unilateral decision at the time, but on Monday admitted that it was intended to benefit the country's Muslim majority, who are observing Ramadan. Delaying the switch to DST meant that sunset would fall at around 6pm rather than 7pm, allowing them to break their daily fast earlier
20 by the clock. He claimed that the relief would have come "without harming any other Lebanese component."

The decision was emblematic of Lebanon's sectarian politics. Its power-sharing rules, dating back to the end of French colonial administration in 1943, divide government
25 posts and public-sector jobs between Muslims and Christians, and originally skewed slightly in favour of Christians. Since Lebanon's civil war, which ended in 1990, such jobs have been divided equally (although Muslims now account for around two-thirds of the population).

end up with ～：最後には ～となる

daylight savings time：サマータイム

emblematic of ～：～を象徴する

as is the custom：慣習に従って

church organisations：教会組織

news outlets：報道機関

caretaker：暫定の

cabinet vote：閣議での投票・決定

albeit ～：～であるが

unilateral：一方的な

observing ～：～の慣習を守る

Ramadan：断食月

relief：安心感

sectarian politics：宗派政治

power-sharing rules：権力分担規則

in favour of ～：～が有利な方に

civil war：内戦

2-52

30   But networks of patronage and clientelism have grown around the two groups. The result is narrow-minded policy. The caretaker education minister, Abbas Halabi, who is known for promoting Muslim-Christian dialogue, said the prime minister had "inflamed sectarian discourse." He said
35 schools would not abide by the (non) change until the law was approved by a cabinet decision. A spokesman for the largest Christian group, the Maronite church, said there had been no consultation on the "surprising" move. Pierre Daher, boss of LBCI, a big broadcaster which also ignored the decree,
40 complained that 48 hours was not enough time to overhaul operations.

    Meanwhile, state-linked institutions toed the line. The two largest telecom companies reminded users to change clock settings manually on their digital devices to avoid the default
45 switch. Middle East Airlines, Lebanon's flagship carrier, advanced all departure times for flights leaving Beirut to keep with international schedules. People struggled with scrambled online calendars, as some appointments were brought forward by an hour, while others stayed unchanged. Double bookings
50 abounded.

    Little wonder, then, that Mr. Mikati was forced to backtrack. The time-zone disruption only added to Lebanon's existing chaos. The country has been in political deadlock since its president left office without a replacement in October. A
55 worsening financial crisis risks spiralling into hyperinflation.

    Fiddling with clocks rarely helps the economy, as Egypt's attempt to cut electricity usage by bringing back DST shows. The quarrel provided Lebanon with a new distraction.

The Economist, March 27, 2023

Vocabulary	
patronage：後援	
clientelism：顧客主義	
"inflamed sectarian discourse"：「扇動された宗派間の言説」	
abide by 〜：〜に従う	
consultation：協議	
LBCI：レバノン国際放送協会	
overhaul operations：業務を点検する	
toed the line：規則に従った	
telecom companies：通信会社	
default switch：デフォルトの切り替え	
advanced 〜：〜を繰り上げた	
abounded：多かった	
disruption：混乱	
without a replacement：後任無しで	
Fiddling with 〜：〜をいじること	
distraction：役に立たない気晴らし	

Exercises

Multiple Choice

次の1～5の英文の質問に答えるために、a～dの中から最も適切なものを1つ選びなさい。

1. Why was the switch to daylight saving time so chaotic?

     a. Most Lebanese had never experienced DST before.
     b. The switch was moved from April to March.
     c. The prime minister suddenly decided to delay the change.
     d. People were told to remain on winter time throughout 2023.

2. What date was finally set for changing their clocks?

     a. March 26th.
     b. March 29th.
     c. April 1st.
     d. April 21st.

3. Which institutions mostly delayed changing to DST?

     a. LBCI.
     b. Churches.
     c. The colonial administration.
     d. Those linked to the government.

4. Why did the sudden policy change create religious tensions?

     a. The government tried helping Muslims without consulting with Christians.
     b. It forced Christians to fast during Ramadan.
     c. International flights to Christian countries were delayed.
     d. It extended the end of the fasting month.

5. Apart from DST confusion, what other problems is Lebanon facing?

     a. Rising prices.
     b. A civil war.
     c. A quarrel with Egypt.
     d. All of the above.

本文の内容に合致するものにＴ（True）、合致しないものにＦ（False）をつけなさい。

(   ) **1.** At first, Mr. Mikati had decided to delay the switch to daylight saving time without giving any reasons.

(   ) **2.** It is Lebanon's custom to set clocks forward to daylight saving time on the final Saturday of March.

(   ) **3.** The Lebanese government disregarded its Christians in helping Muslims who were observing Ramadan.

(   ) **4.** Lebanon's Middle East Airlines set its clock backward.

(   ) **5.** Lebanon is facing the possibility of high inflation.

Vocabulary

次の１〜10の英文は、「time」に関する英文です。日本文に合うように、適切な語を下の語群から１つ選び、（　）内に記入しなさい。

1. 時は金なり。
   Time is (   ).

2. 歳月人を待たず。
   Time and (   ) wait for none.

3. 光陰矢のごとし。
   Time (   ) like an arrow.

4. 失われた時間は２度と戻らない。
   Lost time is never (   ) again.

5. １秒１秒に無限の価値がある。
   Every (   ) is of infinite value.

6. 愛する人にとって時間は永遠だ。
   For those who love, time is (   ).

7. 最も甘美な時間は最も早く過ぎる。
   All our sweetest hours fly (   ).

8. 変えたり影響を与えたりできないものに対して、時間を浪費してはならない。
   Do not waste time on things you cannot change or (   ).

9. 時計に支配されるのではなく、時計を支配しなければならない。
   We must govern the clock, not be (   ) by it.

10. 私たちが持っている最も貴重な資源が時間であることは、実に明らかである。
   It is really clear that the most (   ) resource we all have is time.

eternity	fastest	flies	found	governed
influence	money	precious	second	tide

Unit 23

● カズオ・イシグロ　巨匠黒澤明監督作品をリメイク

ノーベル賞作家カズオ・イシグロ氏による、巨匠黒澤明監督作品のリメーク
『生きる―LIVING』のポスター。ベテラン俳優ビル・ナイの渋さが際立つ
写真：Everett Collection ／アフロ

Before you read

Questions

1. Can you remember which film you saw most recently?

   最近に見た映画を覚えていますか？

2. Do you know who Kazuo Ishiguro is?

   カズオ・イシグロについて知っていますか？

次の1～5の語の説明として最も近いものをa～eから1つ選び、（　）内に記入しなさい。

1. adaptation （　） a. lack of variety or excitement
2. restraint （　） b. approaching or imminent
3. monotony （　） c. new and modified version
4. impending （　） d. control
5. diagnose （　） e. find cause of illness or problem

次の英文は記事の要約です。下の語群から最も適切な語を1つ選び、（　）内に記入しなさい。

2-55

　"Living" is an English-language (　　　　　) of Kurosawa's "Ikiru." Japan-born British writer Kazuo Ishiguro wrote the (　　　　　). He revisits the main theme of (　　　　) meaning at the end of one's life by helping others. But by (　　　　　) the story in London rather than Tokyo he also explores what it (　　　　　) to be a British gentleman in the last years of the empire.

meant　　remake　　screenplay　　seeking　　setting

　2023年1月、アメリカ映画界最高の栄誉とされるアカデミー賞のノミネートが発表された。その中にノーベル文学賞受賞者で日系イギリス人の小説家、カズオ・イシグロがいた。1952年に公開された黒澤明監督の代表作「生きる」を原作にした映画、「LIVING」の脚本を担当し、アカデミー賞の脚色賞にノミネートされた。

　カズオ・イシグロ氏は、1954年、長崎県で日本人の両親の元に生まれたが、海洋学者だった父親が北海油田の調査に参加したことをきっかけに5歳の時にイギリスに移住し、成人した後、イギリス国籍を取得した。小説家として『The Remains of the Day』や『Never Let Me Go』などの作品を発表し、イギリスを代表する作家の1人となった。

　少年時代に見た日本映画は自身のルーツとの重要なつながりとなり、映画「生きる」と出会ったのも、そうした時だった。胃がんで自身の余命が短いことを悟る主人公は、死を突きつけられた絶望感にさいなまれた。男性がたどり着いたのは、残された人生の中で自分に何ができるのかを見つめ直すことだった。『生きる』のテーマは、人生の展望、大事なものとは何か、自分の人生をどう生きるか、ということである。

Reading

2-56

Kazuo Ishiguro discusses remake of iconic Kurosawa film "Ikiru"

KYODO — "Living," a remake set in London of Akira Kurosawa's 1952 classic "Ikiru," has been nominated for best-adapted screenplay and actor in a leading role at the upcoming Academy Awards in Los Angeles.

5   For British author Kazuo Ishiguro, a Nobel-Prize winner born in Nagasaki, writing the adaptation meant delving into what it means to be British, while remaining faithful to the original storyline about a local Japanese official who desperately searches for life's true meaning after being
10 diagnosed with a terminal illness.

2-57

"What was very important to me was this study of the English gentleman. A certain type of Englishness becomes a universal metaphor for something that is inside all human beings," Ishiguro said in a recent online interview. "The need
15 to conform, perhaps a fear of emotions, the frustration of wanting to express yourself but not being able to break out of your professional role, or the role that society has given you."

When he thought about who might play such a role in the adaptation, Ishiguro says he wanted an actor who could show
20 restraint, someone like Chishu Ryu from the late director Yasujiro Ozu's films, and veteran British actor Bill Nighy fit the bill.

2-58

Ishiguro, 68, said that growing up as a boy in London, he was greatly influenced by Kurosawa's original film, starring
25 Takashi Shimura.

In the iconic role played by Shimura, Kanji Watanabe, a city hall civic section chief — an earnest man by all accounts who has not missed a day's work in 30 years — is diagnosed with cancer and told he has little time left to live.

30 Having realized he has led a life of monotony upon facing his impending death, Watanabe makes a last-ditch effort to

Kazuo Ishiguro：カズオ・イシグロ (1954-)《日系英国人ノーベル賞作家》

iconic film：名作

Kurosawa：黒澤明 (1910-98)《代表作に『七人の侍』『羅生門』『どですかでん』など》

"Ikiru"：『生きる』《1952年製作》

"Living"：『生きる─LIVING』

best-adapted screenplay：最優秀脚本賞

actor in a leading role：主演男優賞

adaptation：翻案

delving into ～：～まで掘り下げる

diagnosed with ～：～と診断される

terminal illness：末期の病気

universal metaphor for ～：～の普遍的な隠喩

conform：順応する

restraint：抑制

Chishu Ryu：笠智衆《小津監督作品の常連》

late：故

Yasujiro Ozu：小津安二郎 (1903-63)《代表作品に『東京物語』『晩春』。欧米の監督に熱狂的なファンが多い》

fit the bill：必要条件を満たした

Takashi Shimura：志村喬《黒澤監督作品の常連》

Kanji Watanabe：渡辺完二《役名》

civic section chief：市民課長

by all accounts：誰に聞いても

upon ～：～して

impending：差し迫る

create a playground in his local neighborhood, for which parents had submitted a petition to the city hall for some time, only to have become caught up in red tape and endless
35 referrals.

2-59

The film's last scene is famous for the main character happily singing "Gondola no Uta," a romantic 20th-century Japanese ballad, while swaying on a swing as snow falls in the park he has helped build.

40 "Even if you had a small life with lots of limits, with thought and a big effort, you could make that life wonderful. It could be living to the full. I found this a very liberating message," said Ishiguro, winner of the 2017 Nobel Prize in Literature.

2-60
45 The setting has been recast in post-World War II London.

Although the original story remains, the remake's elegant and refined look is partly down to the setting, which had originally been associated with the black and white images of a more "pessimistic" postwar Japan, now displayed in full,
50 high-definition color and a more optimistic outlook for the future.

Film critic Yuichiro Nishimura said "Living" indeed reminds him of the famous past films of Ozu.

Nishimura added, "Alongside the film's exploration of the
55 twilight of life, there are parallels evoked by the twilight of the shrinking British Empire after the war, which is why Bill Nighy's well-seasoned acting comes alive."

The Japan Times (Kyodo), March 12, 2023

petition：請願

red tape：お役所仕事

endless referrals：たらい回し

"Gondola no Uta"：「ゴンドラの唄」《1915年発表の吉井勇（作詞）による劇中歌。「命短し恋せよ乙女…明日の月日のないものを」で始まる》

small life：ささやかな人生

with thought and 〜：想いと〜があれば

down to 〜：〜に依存している

high definition：高解像度

Yuichiro Nishimura：西村雄一郎

parallels：類似点

well-seasoned：熟練した

comes alive：活き活きしている

Exercises

Multiple Choice

次の1～5の英文の質問に答えるために、a～dの中から最も適切なものを1つ選びなさい。

1. Who appeared in "Ikiru"?

    a. Yasujiro Ozu
    b. Chishu Ryu
    c. Takashi Shimura
    d. Kazuo Ishiguro

2. What is the main storyline of "Living"?

    a. A terminally ill British official searches for life's true meaning.
    b. A Japanese official looks for true happiness before he dies.
    c. A man in the twilight of his life finally finds romance.
    d. A bureaucrat despairs at the destruction that war brought to his city.

3. What does Kanji Watanabe do after being diagnosed with cancer?

    a. He travels from Tokyo to London.
    b. He quits his job and sings romantic ballads.
    c. He creates a playground in his local neighborhood.
    d. He tells parents to submit a petition to the city hall.

4. What message in the original did the writer of the remake find liberating?

    a. Children in cities deserve safe places to play.
    b. Do your job well, however boring it may be.
    c. Enjoy yourself because life is short.
    d. Even a small and limited life can be a great one.

5. In what way does the remake differ from the original?

    a. It deals with the end of life.
    b. It takes place in a small town.
    c. It examines the main character's identity as a gentleman.
    d. It is set in the period after the war.

True or False

本文の内容に合致するものに T （True）、合致しないものに F （False）をつけなさい。

(   )   **1.**   Akira Kurosawa's "Ikiru" has been nominated for best-adapted screenplay at the Academy Awards in Hollywood in 2023.

(   )   **2.**   Kanji Watanabe in "Ikiru" is diagnosed with cancer and told he has little time left to live.

(   )   **3.**   The setting of "Living" was transferred to London after the Second World War.

(   )   **4.**   The appearance of "Ikiru" is associated with high-definition color.

(   )   **5.**   Kanji Watanabe is seen riding on a swing while singing "Gondola no Uta."

Vocabulary

次の 1 ～ 10は、「あの映画は大ヒットした」という意味の英文です。下の語群から最も適切なものを 1 つ選び、（   ）内に記入しなさい。

1.   That movie became the biggest box (   ) hit.

2.   That movie was by far the biggest (   ).

3.   That movie made waves at the (   ) office.

4.   That film was (   ).

5.   That film was a big (   ) at the box office.

6.   That was a one in a (   ) movie.

7.   That movie was a (   ) and there will never be another like it.

8.   That was the best movie of (   ) time.

9.   That was a huge (   ).

10. That film became a (   ) hit.

all	billion	blockbuster	boffo	box
draw	hit	office	one-off	smash

Unit **24**

- 日本がスペインに大金星　新ページを開く
- 際ど過ぎる決勝ゴール判定が論争の的に

2022FIFA ワールドカップ・グループステージでの対スペイン戦で日本が逆転勝利し、決勝トーナメント進出。逆転ゴールをアシストした三苫選手のプレーを巡り、「判定を下すのは誰か？」との問題が議論の的に　　　　写真：新華社／アフロ

Before you read

　a ～ j は、サッカー・フィールドに関する語句です。それぞれ該当するものをイラストの①～⑩の中から選び、（　　）内に記入しなさい。

a. center circle　　　　（　　　）
b. midfield line　　　　（　　　）
c. touch-line　　　　　（　　　）
d. corner kick arc　　　（　　　）
e. penalty area　　　　（　　　）
f. penalty arc　　　　　（　　　）
g. penalty kick mark　　（　　　）
h. goal area　　　　　　（　　　）
i. goal net　　　　　　　（　　　）
j. crossbar　　　　　　　（　　　）

次の１〜５の語の説明として最も近いものをa〜eから１つ選び、（　　）内に記入しなさい。

1. disheartening 　（　　）　**a.** understand
2. click 　（　　）　**b.** function effectively and smoothly
3. point-blank range（　　）　**c.** causing a loss of hope
4. grasp 　（　　）　**d.** close distance
5. notorious 　（　　）　**e.** known for something negative or controversial

Summary

次の英文は記事の要約です。下の語群から最も適切な語を１つ選び、（　　）内に記入しなさい。

2-61

With unexpected (　　　　　　) over Germany and Spain making (　　　　　　) for a disappointing loss against Costa Rica, Japan advanced to the last 16 in Doha. Their winning goal against Spain was controversial as the ball appeared to have gone (　　　　　) of play. The decision to allow the goal (　　　　　) the growing impact of (　　　　　) in soccer.

highlights　　out　　technology　　up　　victories

　　2022年11月20日から12月18日まで行われたサッカーのワールドカップ・カタール大会で、日本は、初戦のドイツに２対１で勝ち、次のクロアチアには０対１で負けたが、強豪スペインを２対１で破り、決勝トーナメント進出を決めた。世界ランキング24位の日本に対し、スペインは７位、ドイツ11位、両チームともワールド・カップ杯優勝の実績がある。その両国を相手に、大金星を２つも挙げた快進撃には、日本のファンたちを驚嘆・感動させた。
　　スペイン戦の決勝点は、堂安選手からのボールを追った三苫選手が左サイドのゴールライン上から折り返し、田中選手が押し込んで逆転した。相手ゴールラインを割りそうだった味方のパスを三苫選手がぎりぎりで追いつき、左足を伸ばしたが、ビデオ判定に持ち込まれた。判定は、三苫選手がクロスを挙げようとしたボールはゴールラインを割っていなかったという判定が出、田中選手の決勝点に結実した。
　　決勝トーナメント１回戦で、日本はPK戦の末、クロアチアに敗れ、悲願の８強入りはかなわなかった。前田選手がゴール前のこぼれ球を押し込んで前半に先制点を奪った。しかし、後半に追いつかれ、１対１のまま延長戦でも決着がつかず、PK戦に持ち込まれ、１対３で敗れ、８強入りはなされなかった。

2-62

Japan adds another thrilling chapter to World Cup story with improbable victory over Spain

improbable：有り得ない

    Japan is in the last 16 of the World Cup after coming from behind to beat former world champions Spain, ranked seventh in the world, and Germany, ranked 11th, to top Group E and set up a showdown with Group F runner-up Croatia.

last 16：ベスト16

showdown：決戦
runner-up：2位の

5   Thursday's result could not have carried the weight it did had the Samurai Blue not written themselves into a corner just four days earlier with a disheartening 1-0 defeat to Costa Rica, seemingly flushing away the momentum built by the team's Nov. 23 win over Germany.

had the Samurai Blue not written 〜：《if を使わない仮定法過去完了》
written themselves into a corner：コーナーに追い込まれる
momentum：勢い

10   Nothing less than a win over Spain would allow Japan to maintain control of its destiny, with a draw leaving fate to chance — or, more precisely, to the other Group E closer between Germany and Los Ticos.

leaving fate to chance：運命を偶然（チャンス）に任せる
closer：（グループの）最終試合
Los Ticos：ロス・ティコス《コスタリカの代表チーム名》

    The Samurai Blue attackers occasionally attempted to
15 press the Spanish back line — with Daizen Maeda utilizing his speed and tenacity — but for the most part focused on the same bend-but-don't-break tactics that served the team well against Germany.

tenacity：粘り強さ
bend-but-don't-break：柔軟な
tactics：戦略

    "In the first half we were focused on forming a defensive
20 block and preventing (Spain captain Sergio) Busquets from creating plays," Maeda said. "From the start of the second half we pressed, and we did it as a team. Everything clicked and it worked well."

preventing 〜 from …：〜に…させない
creating plays：(prevent があるので) プレーさせない
did it as a team：チーム一丸となって戦った
clicked：上手く行った

Don Orlowitz
The Japan Times, December 2, 2022

2-64

Too close to call? Japan's winning goal joins list of controversies

call：判定する

25

    With the game tied at 1-1 through Ritsu Doan's 48th-minute goal and Group E completely up for grabs, Mitoma

up for grabs：どっちが勝つか分からない

raced to meet a low Junya Ito cross from right of the goal and extended his left foot as far as it would go, seemingly willing the ball back into play and centering it for his former Kawasaki Frontale partner-in-crime Tanaka to head home from point-blank range.

Tanaka barely started celebrating before he turned back to see that the linesman had raised his flag, indicating that the ball had gone out of play — only for referee Victor Gomes to signal that a video review was in progress.

The fans at Khalifa International Stadium in Doha also grew silent, soon grasping that the fate of the goal — and perhaps Japan's World Cup aspirations — could ultimately be settled by video assistant referee Fernando Guerrero.

Three minutes later, the "Foot of Mitoma" joined Diego Maradona's 1986 "Hand of God," Frank Lampard's 2010 "ghost goal" and others in the annals of notorious World Cup moments, with professional and armchair pundits alike grasping for explanations and justifications for the decision as Japan took the lead and play resumed.

Although goals such as Maradona's — legendary as they may be — harken back to a time when the referee's word on the pitch was as good as law, Mitoma's pass is emblematic of a new era in which the ruling on the pitch is simply the opening argument. This comes as FIFA redoubles its efforts to reduce officiating-related controversies through the proactive use of technology such as camera arrays and electronic sensors, leading some to wonder whether the sport itself has been irreparably changed as a result.

Don Orlowitz
The Japan Times, December 2, 2022

partner-in-crime：協力者《伊藤のクロスを三苫がライン上で折り返し、田中が得点したことから》

head home from point-blank range：ゴールの至近距離から自陣の方に戻る

Doha：ドーハ《カタールの首都》

settled：決定される

annals：年鑑

pundits：評論家

justifications：正当化

harken back to 〜：〜を思い起こさせる

good：有効な

ruling：裁定

opening argument：議論の元

officiating-related：審判関連の

arrays：配置

irreparably changed：取り返しのつかないほど変化したのではないかと

Exercises

次の１の英文を完成させ、２〜５の英文の質問に答えるために、ａ〜ｄの中から最も適切なものを１つ選びなさい。

1. A tied result against Spain would have meant

    a. Japan's elimination from the World Cup.

    b. Japan advancing to the next round.

    c. Japan winning Group E.

    d. Japan's fate depending on other match results.

2. What was the result of Japan's match against Costa Rica?

    a. 1-0 victory.

    b. 0-1 defeat.

    c. 2-1 victory.

    d. 1-1 draw.

3. What tactics did the Samurai Blue mainly employ against Spain?

    a. Attacking constantly throughout the match.

    b. Exhausting the Spanish with their speed.

    c. Mostly defending in the first half but attacking more in the second.

    d. Shooting at the Spanish goal as often as possible.

4. What was the decision regarding Tanaka's goal after video review?

    a. The goal was awarded.

    b. The goal was disallowed.

    c. The referee awarded a penalty.

    d. The referee declared a tie.

5. What is FIFA's current approach to technology?

    a. It is worried that it will lead to poor decisions.

    b. It has asked all referees to undergo technological training.

    c. It intends to reduce the use of video reviews.

    d. It hopes that video reviews will reduce controversial decisions.

本文の内容に合致するものにT（True）、合致しないものにF（False）をつけなさい。

(   ) **1.** Japan lost to Costa Rica by two goals.

(   ) **2.** The Samurai Blue attacked Spain more in the first half than in the second half.

(   ) **3.** Tanaka's goal was awarded after a video review.

(   ) **4.** Japan's match against Germany ended in an unexpected victory.

(   ) **5.** FIFA is making every effort to reduce the use of video reviews.

Vocabulary

次の1～8は、サッカーに関する英文です。下の語群の中から最も適当な語や語句を1つ選び、（   ）内に記入しなさい。

1. An attacking player attempts to kick the ball past the (   ) team's goalkeeper and between the goalposts to score a goal.

2. A (   ) saved a close-range shot from inside the penalty area.

3. A player takes a free kick, while the opposition form a (   ) in order to try to deflect the ball.

4. A goalkeeper (   ) to stop the ball from (   ) his goal.

5. A (   ) is when the same player makes three goals in one game.

6. Football is a game played between two teams of (   ) players using a round ball.

7. Players are cautioned with a (   ) card, and sent off with a (   ) card.

8. A player scores a penalty kick given after an offence is committed inside the (   ) area.

dives	eleven	entering	goalkeeper	hat trick
opposing	penalty	red	wall	yellow

ニュースメディアの英語

──演習と解説2024年度版──

検印省略	©2024年1月31日　初 版 発 行

編著者　　　　　　　高橋　優身

　　　　　　　　　　伊藤　典子

　　　　　　　Richard Powell

発行者　　　　　　　小川　洋一郎

発行所　　　　　　株式会社朝日出版社

101-0065　東京都千代田区西神田3-3-5
電話 (03) 3239-0271
FAX (03) 3239-0479
e-mail: text-e@asahipress.com
振替口座　00140-2-46008
組版・製版／信毎書籍印刷株式会社

乱丁，落丁本はお取り替えいたします
ISBN 978-4-255-15712-2 C1082